· BROWN ·

· B R O W N ·

The Last Discovery of America

RICHARD RODRIGUEZ

■ ■ ■

Viking

VIKING
Published by the Penguin Group
Penguin Putnam Inc., 375 Hudson Street, New York, New York 10014, U.S.A.
Penguin Books Ltd, 80 Strand, London WC2R 0RL, England
Penguin Books Australia Ltd, 250 Camberwell Road, Camberwell,
 Victoria 3124, Australia
Penguin Books Canada Ltd, 10 Alcorn Avenue,
 Toronto, Ontario, Canada M4V 3B2
Penguin Books India (P) Ltd, 11 Community Centre, Panchsheel Park,
 New Delhi–110 017, India
Penguin Books (N.Z.) Ltd, Cnr Rosedale and Airborne Roads, Albany,
 Auckland, New Zealand
Penguin Books (South Africa) (Pty) Ltd, 24 Sturdee Avenue,
 Rosebank, Johannesburg 2196, South Africa

Penguin Books Ltd, Registered Offices:
Harmondsworth, Middlesex, England

First published in 2002 by Viking Penguin,
a member of Penguin Putnam Inc.

10 9 8 7 6 5 4 3 2 1

Page 233 constitutes an extension of this copyright page.

LIBRARY OF CONGRESS CATALOGING-IN-PUBLICATION DATA
Rodriguez, Richard.
 Brown : the last discovery of America / Richard Rodriguez.
  p. cm.
  ISBN 0-670-03043-0
   1. Hispanic Americans—Race identity.   2. Hispanic Americans—
History.   3. Racially mixed people—United States—Race identity.
4. Racially mixed people—United States—History.   5. United States—
Race relations.   6. United States—Race relations—Psychological aspects.
7. Erotica—United States—Psychological aspects.   8. Rodriguez, Richard.
9. Mexican Americans—Biography.   I. Title.

E184.S75 R67 2002
305.868073—dc21   2001057919

This book is printed on acid-free paper. ∞

Printed in the United States of America
Set in Fairfield with Didot display
Designed by Carla Bolte

For Jimmy, before the birds cry . . .

Preface

BROWN AS IMPURITY.

I write of a color that is not a singular color, not a strict recipe, not an expected result, but a color produced by careless
desire, even by accident; by two or several. I write of blood that
is blended. I write of brown as complete freedom of substance
and narrative. I extol impurity.

I eulogize a literature that is suffused with brown, with allusion, irony, parodox—ha!—pleasure.

I write about race in America in hopes of undermining the
notion of race in America.

Brown bleeds through the straight line, unstaunchable—the
line separating black from white, for example. Brown confuses.
Brown forms at the border of contradiction (the ability of language to express two or several things at once, the ability of bodies to experience two or several things at once).

It is that brown faculty I uphold by attempting to write
brownly. And I defy anyone who tries to unblend me or to say
what is appropriate to my voice.

You will often find brown in this book as the cement between leaves of paradox.

You may not want paradox in a book. In which case, you had better seek a pure author.

Brown is the color most people in the United States associate with Latin America.

Apart from stool sample, there is no browner smear in the American imagination than the Rio Grande. No adjective has attached itself more often to the Mexican in America than "dirty"—which I assume gropes toward the simile "dirt-like," indicating dense concentrations of melanin.

I am dirty, all right. In Latin America, what makes me brown is that I am made of the conquistador and the Indian. My brown is a reminder of conflict.

And of reconciliation.

In my own mind, what makes me brown in the United States is that I am Richard Rodriguez. My baptismal name and my surname marry England and Spain, Renaissance rivals.

North of the U.S.–Mexico border, brown appears as the color of the future. The adjective accelerates, becomes a verb: "America is browning." South of the border, brown sinks back into time. Brown is time.

In middle chapters, I discuss the ways Hispanics brown an America that traditionally has chosen to describe itself as black-and-white. I salute Richard Nixon, the dark father of Hispanicity. But my Hispanic chapters, as I think of them—the chapters I originally supposed were going to appear first in this book—gave way to more elementary considerations. I mean the meeting of the Indian, the African, and the European in colonial America. Red. Black. White. The founding palette.

Some months ago, a renowned American sociologist predicted to me that Hispanics will become "the new Italians" of the United States. (What the Sicilian had been for nineteenth-century America, the Colombian would become for the twenty-first century.)

His prediction seems to me insufficient because it does not account for the influence of Hispanics on the geography of the American imagination. Because of Hispanics, Americans are coming to see the United States in terms of a latitudinal vector, in terms of south-north, hot-cold; a new way of placing ourselves in the twenty-first century.

America has traditionally chosen to describe itself as an east-west country. I grew up on the east-west map of America, facing east. I no longer find myself so easily on that map. In middle age (also brown, its mixture of loss and capture), I end up on the shore where Sir Francis Drake first stepped onto California. I look toward Asia.

As much as I celebrate the browning of America (and I do), I do not propose an easy optimism. The book's last chapter was completed before the events of September 11, 2001, and now will never be complete. The chapter describes the combustible dangers of brown; the chapter annotates the tragedies it anticipated.

I think brown marks a reunion of peoples, an end to ancient wanderings. Rival cultures and creeds conspire with Spring to create children of a beauty, perhaps of a harmony, previously unknown. Or long forgotten. Even so, the terrorist and the skinhead dream in solitude of purity and of the straight line because they fear a future that does not isolate them. In a brown future, the most dangerous actor might likely be the cosmopolite, conversant in alternate currents, literatures, computer programs. The cosmopolite may come to hate his brownness, his facility, his indistinction, his mixture; the cosmopolite may yearn for a thorough religion, ideology, or tribe.

Many days, I left my book to wander the city, to discover the city outside my book was comically browning. Walking down Fillmore Street one afternoon, I was enjoying the smell of salt, the brindled pigeons, brindled light, when a conversation overtook me, parted around me, just as I passed the bird-store window: Two girls. Perhaps sixteen. White, Anglo, whatever. Tottering on their silly shoes. Talking of boys. The one girl saying to the other: . . . *His complexion is so cool, this sort of light—well, not that light* . . .

I realized my book will never be equal to the play of the young.

. . . *Sort of reddish brown, you know* . . . The other girl nodded, readily indicated that she did know. But still Connoisseur Number One sought to bag her simile. . . . *Like a Sugar Daddy bar—you know that candy bar?*

Two decades ago, I wrote *Hunger of Memory,* the autobiography of a scholarship boy. Ten years later, in *Days of Obligation,* I wrote about the influence of Mexican ethnicity on my American life. This volume completes a trilogy on American public life and my private life. *Brown* returns me to years I have earlier described. I believe it is possible to describe a single life thrice, if from three isolations: *Class. Ethnicity. Race.*

When I began this book, I knew some readers would take "race" for a tragic noun, a synonym for conflict and isolation. Race is not such a terrible word for me. Maybe because I am skeptical by nature. Maybe because my nature is already mixed. The word race encourages me to remember the influence of eroticism on history. For that is what race memorializes. Within any discussion of race, there lurks the possibility of romance.

Contents

Preface xi

CHAPTER

One The Triad of Alexis de Tocqueville 1

Two In the Brown Study 33

Three The Prince and I 47

Four Poor Richard 81

Five Hispanic 103

Six The Third Man 125

Seven Dreams of a Temperate People 145

Eight Gone West 169

Nine Peter's Avocado 193

Acknowledgments 231

· B R O W N ·

- *Chapter One* -

THE TRIAD OF
ALEXIS DE TOCQUEVILLE

TWO WOMEN AND A CHILD IN A GLADE BESIDE A SPRING.
Beyond them, the varnished wilderness wherein bright birds
cry. The child is chalk, Europe's daughter. Her dusky atten-
dants, a green Indian and a maroon slave.

The scene, from *Democracy in America,* is discovered by
that most famous European traveler to the New World, Alexis
de Tocqueville, aristocratic son of the Enlightenment, liberal,
sickly, gray, violet, lacking the vigor of the experiment he has
set himself to observe.

"I remember . . . I was traveling through the forests which
still cover the state of Alabama. . . ."

In a clearing, at some distance, an Indian woman appears
first to Monsieur, followed by a "Negress," holding by the hand
"a little white girl of five or six years."

The Indian: "A sort of barbarous luxury" set off her costume;

I

"rings of metal were hanging from her nostrils and ears, her hair, which was adorned with glass beads, fell loosely upon her shoulders. . . ." The Negress wore "squalid European garments."

Such garments are motifs of de Tocqueville's pathos. His description intends to show the African and the Indian doomed by history in corresponding but opposing ways. (History is a coat cut only to the European.)

"The young Indian, taking the child in her arms, lavished upon her such fond caresses as mothers give, while the Negress endeavored, by various little artifices, to attract the [child's] attention. . . ."

The white child "displayed in her slightest gestures a consciousness of superiority that formed a strange contrast with her infantine weakness; as if she received the attentions of her companions with a sort of condescension."

Thus composed: The Indian. The Negress. The white child.

". . . In the picture that I have just been describing there was something peculiarly touching; a bond of affection here united the oppressors with the oppressed, and the effort of Nature to bring them together rendered still more striking the immense distance placed between them by prejudice and the laws."

At Monsieur's approach, this natural colloquy is broken. He becomes the agent of history. Seeing him, the Indian suddenly rises, "push[es] the child roughly away and, giving [Monsieur] an angry look, plunge[s] into the thicket."

The Negress rests; awaits de Tocqueville's approach.

Neither response satisfies the European. The African, de Tocqueville writes, has lost the memory of ancestors, of custom and tongue; the African has experienced degradation to his very soul, has become a true slave. "Violence made him a slave, and the habit of servitude gives him the thoughts and desires of a slave; he admires his tyrants more than he hates them, and finds his joy and his pride in the servile imitation of those who oppress him."

The bejeweled Indian, alternately, is "condemned . . . to a wandering life, full of inexpressible sufferings," because European interlopers have unbalanced the provender of Nature.

And, de Tocqueville remarks (a fondness for fable), whereas the Negro's response to mistreatment is canine, the Indian's is feline. "The Negro makes a thousand fruitless efforts to insinuate himself among men who repulse him. . . ." The Indian is filled with diffidence toward the white, "has his imagination inflated with the pretended nobility of his origin, and lives and dies in the midst of these dreams of pride." The Indian refuses civilization; the African slave is rendered unfit for it.

But cher Monsieur: You saw the Indian sitting beside the African on a drape of baize. They were easy together. The sight of them together does not lead you to wonder about a history in which you are not the narrator?

These women are but parables of your interest in yourself. Rather than consider the nature of their intimacy, you are preoccupied alone with the meaning of your intrusion. You in your dusty leather boots, cobbled on the rue du Faubourg

St.-Honoré. Your tarnished silver snuffbox, your saddlebag filled with the more ancient dust of books. You in your soiled cambric. Vous-même.

▪ ▪ ▪

A boy named Buddy came up beside me in the schoolyard. I don't remember what passed as prologue, but I do not forget what Buddy divulged to me:

If you're white, you're all right;
If you're brown, stick around;
If you're black, stand back.

It was as though Buddy had taken me to a mountaintop and shown me the way things lay in the city below.

In Sacramento, my brown was not halfway between black and white. On the leafy streets, on the east side of town, where my family lived, where Asians did not live, where Negroes did not live, my family's Mexican shades passed as various. We did not pass "for" white; my family passed among white, as in one of those old cartoons where Clarabelle the Cow goes shopping downtown and the mercantile class of dogs does not remark her exception. As opposed to Amos and Andy, whose downtown was a parallel universe of no possible admixture. And as I easily pass in these pages between being an American and regarding America from a distance.

As opposed, also, to the famous photograph of a girl in Little Rock in the pages of *Life* magazine. A black girl, no older than Alice, must pass alone through the looking glass. I remember wondering what my brown would have meant to Little Rock, how my brown would have withstood Little Rock.

In the Sacramento of the 1950s, it was as though White simply hadn't had time enough to figure Brown out. It was a busy white time. Brown was like the skinny or fat kids left over after the team captains chose sides. "You take the rest"—my cue to wander away to the sidelines, to wander away.

In those years, I recall seeing a movie called *The Defiant Ones*. Two convicts—Sidney Poitier and Tony Curtis—were shackled to each other. The movie did not occur to me racially or politically but erotically. The child's obvious question concerned privacy. By comparison, the pairing of the Lone Ranger and Tonto on television did occur to me racially. They were twin scourges, upholders of the law of the West. They were of compatible mind and they were of complementary skill—one sneaky, one full-charge. I noticed Tonto had no vocabulary but gravitas. Of more immediate interest to me was that each wore the symbol of his reserved emotion—the mask; the hair in a bun. I didn't identify with Tonto any more than with Lone, or less. I identified with their pairing.

My parents had come from Mexico, a short road in my imagination. I felt myself as coming from a caramelized planet, an upside-down planet, pineapple-cratered. Though I was born here, I came from the other side of the looking glass, as did Alice, though not alone like Alice. Downtown I saw lots of brown people. Old men on benches. Winks from Filipinos. Sikhs who worked in the fields were the most mysterious brown men, their heads wrapped in turbans. They were the rose men. They

looked like roses. And the Palestinian communist bookie—
entirely hearsay—who ran a tobacco store of pungent brownness (the smell of rum-soaked cigars and cheap, cherry-scented
pipe tobacco) was himself as brown as a rolled cigar, but the
more mysterious for having been born in Bethlehem.

And as we passed, we passed very close to the young man,
close enough for me to smell him, something anointing his
hair. He was the most beautiful man (my first consciousness of
the necessity for oxymoron) I remember seeing as a boy. He
wore a suit-vest over his naked torso. He wore a woman's gold
locket, with a dark red stone. He was petting a dog in the
street. His pant knees were dirty. He smelled of coconut. He
smiled brilliantly as we passed.

The missing tooth.

Heepsie, my mother whispered, taking me firmly by the
hand, refusing his blazing notice with an averted nod.

I had seen the gypsy's mother—she must be his mother—
dozens of times, sitting on a lawn chair outside her "office" on
H Street, near my father's work. There was a sign in the window beneath which she sat, a blank hand outlined in neon.
She never sought or met my gaze. She looked Mexican to me.
Not Mexican, my parents assured me. My brother said, *Watch
out, Ricky, she's sitting there reading your tombstone.*

A boy with a face as dark as mine, but several years older,
stepped out of the crowd at the state fair to press a warm dime
into my hand. Said nothing; wanted nothing, apparently; disappeared. His curious solemnity. But I interpreted—because I
remember—the transaction as one of brown eyes.

A friend of mine, born and raised in Hong Kong, remembers attending British schools in Hong Kong; remembers being constrained to learn about India. My friend learned nothing about China; instead, the Gita and *Only connect*, Lord Curzon, Mother Ganga, mulligatawny, Mahatma Gandhi. The British obsession with India—as its existential opposite—seemed to my friend an affront to China. But surely there was also a kind of freedom in growing up without the Briton's attention?

My uncle from India was several times called "nigger" by strangers downtown in Sacramento. His daughter, Delia, forbade the rhyme I learned at school. *Eenie, meenie, mynie, moe. . . .* But her eyes softened as she corrected me and her mouth softened.

Brown is a bit of a cave in my memory. Like Delia's eyes.

Lights up, then, on "Theme from a Summer Place," on blue and gold and electric guitar strings. A decade on. I am staying for a month of summer in Laguna Beach with the family of my best friend, Larry Faherty. I am covered with a cool film of Sea & Ski, as is Larry, though I suspect the insistence on this precaution by Larry's mother is gratuitous in my case. Larry's mother is sitting on the deck with a neighbor, a red-faced woman with protuberant pale blue eyes, penciled eyebrows. The bug-eyed woman burbles into her tomato juice cocktail, "some niggers . . ." (ah, ah, ah, I can feel the hairs lift on the back of my neck) ". . . some niggers came onto the beach over the weekend . . ." (she glances at me while she is saying this; her eyes are needles; I am the camel) ". . . we let them know they weren't welcome." It is not clear where I fit into her use of the first-person plural. Finally, however, my presence does not disturb her narrative.

Years later, the same story, a different summer—Columbia, South Carolina. A different storyteller—a lawyer in New York rehearses his famous anecdote, "The Hawaiian Stranger," in three passages; two tumblers of scotch.

1. It is summer, 1944; World War II is coming to an end. (There is no tragic coast to this story; the boys in it will not taste the tin can of death.) The lawyer's mother, gallantly streaming, has decided to invite a bevy of "boys so far from home" from a nearby army base onto her lawn for a Fourth of July picnic. Of course a complement of young ladies has been invited as well, Sallys and Dorothys, women from town and from the college.

2. The day dawns golden. Syrup and mosquitoes. The hired help arrive first, disinterested capable hands. By and by, the young men arrive. Smiles, sweat rings, aftershave. The young women arrive also, in summer dresses. There will be games to put the gentlemen at ease. The women arrange themselves in wicker chairs, sip cool drinks and appraise the gentlemen from the shade of the porch.

Volleyball.

But, "South Carolina in summer . . . ," the lawyer sighs, five decades later, rattling the ice in his glass.

3. Scotch #2. Conspicuous among the young recruits is a tall brown man with short-cropped hair. The Hawaiian. "Poor Mama. 'Another Coca-Cola, Mr. Cooke?' (She could just about manage that one.) But, during the volleyball game, Mr. Cooke sheds first his shirt, then his T-shirt." The narrator remembers the

sight of brown shoulders, brown nipples, a navel that tempted vertigo—"Why do we remember such things, and not who invented the cotton gin?"—and the sweat streaming down Mr. Cooke's rib cage; his flared nostrils.

(*Poor Mama.*)

Poor Narrator. Nevertheless, Mama keeps her stride, marching her fruit-bobbling sandals into the house and back out to the yard. More potato salad? Key lime pie. Lemonade. "Each time she'd pass me—I was sitting alone under the shade tree—she'd detour; she'd come around the trunk of the tree, bend down so close I could smell her powder—she pretended to be fixing my collar or working on my cowlick—but her whisper came down furious as a flyswatter: 'He isn't either a nigger, you mind yourself, he's Hawaiian.'"

Stories darken with time, some of them.

▪ ▪ ▪

The first book by an African American I read was Carl T. Rowan's memoir, *Go South to Sorrow*. I found it on the bookshelf at the back of my fifth-grade classroom, an adult book. I can remember the quality of the morning on which I read. It was a sunlit morning in January, a Saturday morning, cold, high, empty. I sat in a rectangle of sunlight, near the grate of the floor heater in the yellow bedroom. And as I read, I became aware of warmth and comfort and optimism. I was made aware of my comfort by the knowledge that others were not, are not, comforted. Carl Rowan at my age was not comforted. The sensation was pleasurable.

Only a few weeks ago, in the year in which I write, Carl T.

Rowan died. Hearing the news, I felt the sadness one feels when a writer dies, a writer one claims as one's own—as potent a sense of implication as for the loss of a body one has known. Over the years, I had seen Rowan on TV. He was not, of course he was not, the young man who had been with me by the heater—the photograph on the book jacket, the voice that spoke through my eyes. The muscles of my body must form the words and the chemicals of my comprehension must form the words, the windows, the doors, the Saturdays, the turning pages of another life, a life simultaneous with mine.

It is a kind of possession, reading. Willing the Other to abide in your present. His voice, mixed with sunlight, mixed with Saturday, mixed with my going to bed and then getting up, with the pattern and texture of the blanket, with the envelope from a telephone bill I used as a bookmark. With going to Mass. With going to the toilet. With my mother in the kitchen, with whatever happened that day and the next; with clouds forming over the Central Valley, with the flannel shirt I wore, with what I liked for dinner, with what was playing at the Alhambra The-ater. I remember Carl T. Rowan, in other words, as myself, as I was. Perhaps that is what one mourns.

▪ ▪ ▪

In the Clunie Public Library in Sacramento, in those last years of a legally segregated America, there was no segregated shelf for Negro writers. Frederick Douglass on the same casement with Alexis de Tocqueville, Benjamin Franklin. Today, when our habit is willfully to confuse literature with sociology, with sorting, with trading in skins, we imagine the point of a "life" is to address some sort of numerical average, common obstacle or persecution. Here is a book "about" teenaged Chinese-American girls. So it is shelved.

I found this advice, the other day, in an essay by Joseph Addison, his first essay for the *Spectator,* the London journal, Thursday, March 1, 1711. "I have observed, that a reader seldom puruses a Book with Pleasure, 'til he knows the writer of it be a black or a fair Man, of a mild or cholerick Disposition, Married or a Bachelor, with other particulars of the like nature, that conduce very much to the right understanding of an Author. To gratifie this Curiosity, which is so natural to a Reader. . . ."

It is one thing to know your author—man or woman or gay or black or paraplegic or president. It is another thing to choose only man or woman or et cetera, as the only quality of voice empowered to address you, as the only class of sensibility or experience able to understand you, or that you are able to understand.

How a society orders its bookshelves is as telling as the books a society writes and reads. American bookshelves of the twenty-first century describe fractiousness, reduction, hurt. Books are isolated from one another, like gardenias or peaches, lest they bruise or become bruised, or, worse, consort, confuse. If a man in a wheelchair writes his life, his book will be parked in a blue-crossed zone: "Self-Help" or "Health." There is no shelf for bitterness. No shelf for redemption. The professor of Romance languages at Dresden, a convert to Protestantism, was tortured by the Nazis as a Jew—only that—a Jew. His book, published sixty years after the events it recounts, is shelved in my neighborhood bookstore as "Judaica." There is no shelf for irony.

Books should confuse. Literature abhors the typical. Literature flows to the particular, the mundane, the greasiness of paper, the taste of warm beer, the smell of onion or quince. Auden has a line: "Ports have names they call the sea." Just so will literature describe life familiarly, regionally, in terms life is accustomed to use—high or low matters not. Literature cannot by this impulse betray the grandeur of its subject—there is only one subject: What it feels like to be alive. Nothing is irrelevant. Nothing is typical.

It was only from the particular life—a single life, a singular voice named Frederick Douglass, a handsome man, anybody can see that, a tall man, a handsome man, who lived and died in another century, another place, another skin, another light, the light changing every hour, every day, within a room; he did not choose the room or the hour or the skin—that a brown boy in Sacramento could sense the universality of dissimilarity. The offense of slavery (the lure of literature) was that Douglass's life was precisely different from mine in California, a century later.

Now I am a writer, and now that my writing so often runs close to the boundaries of social science, I must remember it is the reader alone who decides a book's universality. One cannot arrange a classic. It is the reader's life that opens a book. I am dead. Only a reader can testify to the ability of literature to open; sometimes this opening causes pain.

I mean to put you in company with the young African-

American girl who discovers she is like Jane Austen. How so? In temperament, in sensibility, in some way she recognizes and approves. Then this thrilling recognition brings a cloud of shame to her spontaneity—I write of myself, of course—shame for what she intuits, shame for what she cannot share: that a novel from some unenlightened world is not fit for her. She is discouraged. Why it is unfit she cannot completely account for. (Because the sensibility she reads would be cruelly amused at the spectacle of her interest?) She notices her absence. Another girl her age, or a girl from another age, would not notice; would not need to notice.

The nescience of a book can undermine its clarity, can spoil our pleasure in it. Our age looks for exclusion. And there is a certain gumption missing from our age as a result, and from the literature of our age.

Helen Keller wrote that dust spoiled the feel of things for her. Simone Weil wrote that the music and the pageantry of a Nazi youth parade were viscerally thrilling to her.

Already in grammar school there were rooms in my reading life into which I would have been reluctant to admit Frederick Douglass, for I knew in those rooms he was mocked. *You must wait here, Mr. Douglass.* I made myself the go-between. I must come to the conclusion that the suite of mockery, though refined, though pleasing to me in most ways—a room of Thackeray's perhaps—retained poisonous vapors of another age, and would not have admitted me. And yet these apartments existed uniquely in my imagination, nowhere else. In books, you say. But books must be reimagined, misunderstood, read. Readers repair to books as men and women to monasteries, none with an identical motive. I was the reader of Thackeray. These rooms, these weathers, these confidences from the dust must burn my ears if they were read out loud. But in my privacy I could regret they could not be revised. I strained to restore them to the conditional. Clouds that might pass. The authors could not know what Frederick Douglass would have taught them. Were they damned? Was the crudeness of their imaginations commensurate with the way they made toast? Were books a sort of limbo, characterized by unchangeability? Books! They were damned, authors, not to know that what they dropped could not be revised.

I did not know until this year that Keats spoke with a cockney accent.

▪ ▪ ▪

My reading was a thicket, a blind, from which I observed. (Addison: "Thus I live in the world, rather as a spectator of mankind than as one of the species. . . .")

A scholarship boy, and sexually secretive, I was deaf to the rock-n-roll blaring from the radio. I did not know that the great drama of integration—White with Black—was playing itself out under the guise of the Top 40. I did not realize, as my younger sister did—she watched Dick Clark's *American Bandstand* each afternoon—that whites were emancipating themselves by dancing to Little Richard. I do remember that song called "The Name Game"—my sister could do it, I never could—in which an African-American voice (*Come on now, you try it . . .*)

cheerfully played havoc with the American tongue. I remember laughing, dizzied by the freedom of the voice to play.

The Indian plunges into the thicket. The Negress awaits the white man's approach.

That part of America where I felt least certain about the meaning of my brown skin was also the part of the country I came to know best in my reading.

While my sister danced, I sat on shellacked benches on the Colored side of the Memphis bus station, felt underneath with my hand for dried gum. I drank from the Colored fountain. The fountain tasted of rust, and rust stained the basin and made it unpleasant. I could see where the White fountain was. There was no one about. I was human. I was thirsty. I was quick. As I bent my head to the fount, a hand grabbed me from behind, pulled back my head by its hair, my arms flaying for a purchase on my tormentor. I felt the knuckle—Oh my Jesus, I felt the gold ring boring into my scalp. I knew the ring from a thousand observations. I had seen it setting down coin, raising a glass, grasping the reins of that red-eyed bay. I had seen it, often enough, raised in anger. I said his name out loud, *Please, mister. . . .* (All I know of life is this: Hair is amazingly strong, and I went with my hair, backward. If I had parted from my hair, I might have saved my life.)

While my sister danced, I watched Malcolm X interviewed on KCRA-TV, Sacramento. I noticed a fierceness in him and a criticism of White that made no distinction between good readers and bad. Something in his manner, something I recognized, rhymed with the scholarship boy I was.

I went alone. My evenings out in Sacramento were secretive. Insofar as they were experiments with adulthood, I wouldn't have considered bringing anyone else along. I went to hear Malcolm X alone, as I went alone to hear Marian Anderson. (Her red velvet gown. A baby's little blue cry pierced the golden disk she had spun. Silence. Shame for Sacramento! A nod to her pianist to resume.) When I went to hear Malcolm X, I felt as invisible, as anonymous, as safe as I have ever felt. The audience was overwhelmingly male. It was a busy black time. No one seemed to notice my brown in the crowd.

Malcolm X stood in a circle of light. He was not possessed of a theatrical power to transfigure himself. His voice was nothing at all like what I expected. I expected the near-singing of ministers I had heard broadcast from the South. His voice was high, nasal, a scold's voice. A hickory stick. But for all his thin stricture, there was something generous about this man, something of Benjamin Franklin—his call to brothers to better themselves. In his black mortician's suit, Malcolm X spoke of his early life, his years as a con, a hustler; cruel toward women because false to himself. His glasses flared in the spotlight.

What about that summer night was so thrilling to me?

▪ ▪ ▪

There is shattered glass in the street. I am transported by James Baldwin to Harlem in the aftermath of a race riot. ("On the morning of the 3rd of August, we drove my father to the graveyard through a wilderness of smashed plate glass.") Among

Baldwin's plays, I knew only *The Amen Corner* (Beah Richards played it in San Francisco). Among the novels, I favored *Go Tell It on the Mountain*. Most, I loved Baldwin's essays. There was to a Baldwin essay a metropolitan elegance I envied, a refusal of the livid. In Baldwin I found a readiness to rise to prophetic wrath, something like those ministers, and yet, once more, to bend down in tenderness, to call grown men and women "baby" (a whiff of the theater). Watching Baldwin on television—I will always consider the fifties to have been a sophisticated time— fixed for me what being a writer must mean. Arching eyebrows intercepted ironies, parenthetically declared fouls; mouthfuls of cigarette smoke shot forth ribbons of exactitude.

▪ ▪ ▪

The Freedom March of 1965, from Selma to Montgomery, marked the turning point for the Civil Rights movement in the South. It became clear to America that the spiritual momentum of the march would carry the day; the South would bend.

Then the Negro Civil Rights movement, the slow sad movement of moral example, veered north, cooled, hardened as it climbed, to a secular anger. The Watts riots in Los Angeles of 1965 were the worst U.S. riots in twenty years. Young Negroes with no time to waste, no patience for eternal justice, renamed themselves "black." Their proclamation began a project of redefinition, not only of themselves and of their political movement, but of power, of glamour. The Name Game was at once fierce and dazzling. Black America led white America through the changes. The equation of desire was going to be reversed.

Within the new insistence on blackness was a determination on the part of blacks to transform into boast all that whites had, for generations, made jest: curly hair, orange polyester, complexion, dialect, spiritual ecstasy.

When I was in high school, white boys inhaled black voices like helium. The Christian Brothers' Gaels drove off to a football game in the big yellow bus, windows lowered, the crewcuts singing a Little Stevie Wonder song in falsetto for the pure pleasure and novelty of squeezing their thighs to the highest pitch.

But the necessity, for a new black generation, of transposing shame into pride led to a dangerous romanticism. Segregation, de facto and legal, was transformed into self-willed exclusion—also a point of pride. Perhaps it was that the Negro Civil Rights movement of the South had been governed by a Protestant faith in conversion, whereas the northern black movement cared nothing for conversion.

▪ ▪ ▪

Despite laws prohibiting black literacy in the nineteenth century, the African in America took the paper-white English and remade it (as the Irish and the Welsh also took their English), wadded it up, rigmarolled it, rewound it into a llareggub rap, making English theirs, making it idiosyncratically glamorous (*Come on now, you try it*), making it impossible for any American to use English henceforward without remembering them; making English so cool, so jet, so festival, that children want it only that way.

The only voices as blatant as black voices, as contentious, as alive in American air and literature, are those first-generation Jewish voices, skeptical, playful, dicing every assertion. The black-Jewish conversation was inevitable, for reasons of rhetoric, of history, of soul. As the American Indian had also been drawn, the Jew must have felt drawn to the African American from some recognition of exclusion, expectation of exclusion. Unlike the Indian, however, the Jew had been shaped by a theology of the Word—a schooling that became, like the African's, a strategy for survival. And for a time, theirs was a brilliant alliance, the Black with the Jew. But the genius for verbal survival uniting Black and Jew would undermine their alliance.

"You cannot imagine how many times I need to squirt my eyes with Visine just to get through *Othello*. (So rage won't dry them out.)" An African-American graduate student addressed a roomful of English professors and graduate students at Berkeley. (This was late in the 1970s.) A Jewish professor immediately joined with "You can't imagine how difficult it is for me to read *The Merchant of Venice*" (assuming the alliance).

"Well, goddamn!" snarled the black woman in a stage whisper, her topknot vibrating, her eyes lashed to the notebook on her desk, "Jews always have to feel exactly what we are feeling, only more so."

▪ ▪ ▪

Did you ever cross over to Snedens . . . ?

Snedens Landing is a pre-revolutionary town upstate. I was fifty before I heard a recording of Mabel Mercer singing that brittle song. I don't care for the song. I like Mabel Mercer. She was a black Englishwoman who grew up in a theatrical family. She went to Paris at nineteen; she sang in bars, mainly for expatriate audiences, James Baldwin and others. From Paris, Mabel Mercer came to New York, became a fixture of the supper clubs there. She sat in a straight-backed chair, in a spotlight, her hands folded in her lap. She leaned slightly forward, as if imparting a confidence to her audience. The confidence she imparted was that hers was the most refined lyric sensibility in Manhattan of the 1950s.

Mabel Mercer performed the songs of Porter and Coward and such with a perfect mid-Atlantic pronunciation, which is to say, without a trace of melanin in her voice. This was not ventriloquism or minstrelsy or parody—I was disappointed to learn it wasn't—but the voice was authentic to Mercer because she had been educated by British nuns who insisted upon public-school elocution. Another cabaret singer of that time, Anita O'Day, quoted in a book I can't find, described Mabel Mercer thus: "That chick has the weirdest fucking act in show business."

I would like my act to be as weird. An old brown man walking the beach, singing "The Love Song of J. Alfred Prufrock." I have, throughout my writing life, pondered what a brown voice should sound like.

I have pondered what a black voice should sound like.

On September 16, 1966—contemporary newspaper accounts reported a cool evening—the new Metropolitan Opera House opened in New York City. President Johnson and Mrs. Johnson were in attendance, as were President and Mrs. Marcos of the Philippines, as was U Thant, Secretary-General of the United Nations. The opera house, designed by Wallace K. Harrison, was a modernist pavilion with an arched façade, retractable chandeliers, murals by Marc Chagall. The opera commissioned for the opening was *Antony and Cleopatra* by American composer Samuel Barber. Leontyne Price sang the role of Cleopatra. The Franco Zeffirelli production fused disparate motifs of colonial adventure in the manner of a seventeenth-century print. Zeffirelli's Egyptians were Elizabethan-Floridian. Leontyne Price wore an enormous feathered, beribboned headdress reminiscent of Amazonia, and a gown of Renaissance cut. She was costumed to appear bare-breasted, a caryatid of continental allegory—at once the African and the Indian of Alexis de Tocqueville's notice. At least that is how I remember the photograph of Leontyne Price in *Time* magazine; that is the image that comes to mind as I reread de Tocqueville.

You are probably too young to remember or perhaps you have forgotten what a pride for America that evening was—the most modern opera house in the world to prolong the heartbeat of the nineteenth century, and with Leontyne Price, the reigning dramatic soprano of her day, enshrined at the center. And yet, the Metropolitan Opera seemed at that moment—eight o'clock, September 16, 1966—to mark the very crossroads of American history, the division of the old era and the new. Leontyne Price seemed the apotheosis of African America, of new America, as if uncountable degradations inflicted upon

African Americans might be ransomed by a single, soaring human voice.

That same year, 1966, there were thirty-eight race riots in American cities. And thirty-five years later, Lincoln Center looks irrelevant; there is talk in the papers about pulling it down.

That same year, 1966, I was in college. I typed, on erasable onionskin paper: "White southern writers had earlier preoccupied themselves with the deconstruction of the South along Grecian lines, a lament for pride brought low and a contrition for the sins of the Fathers, all the while insisting upon kinship—the black maid's sigh, the white child's 'Why?'"

Black maid's sigh? White child's Why?

My forehead began to pain me remarkably, to throb; a sort of mockery seized upon my temples, then billowed from my ears, like black smoke from a stovepipe. A figment stood before me:

Naw.
Listen, Hiawatha, honey, sittin by yo heatah,
Cradlin' little ninny books, playin' Little Eva—
Doodah mantchuns fulla haunted crackahs,
Long-face mens pullin' sacks a 'baccas,
Clean white aprons wid dese fairytale patchas!
The sky is the skin o' yo eye, Hiawatha!
Peel that skin off yo eye!

The figment was clothed with a red calico shirt and a voluminous apron with many pockets and colored patches sewn on, like the patches on jerkins and pinafores in a child's picture

book. It wore a sort of turban on its head. The head was a ta-
blespoonful of black wax, the size of a chunk of coal. It had
eyes—large, lidless sclera with black balls painted in. But no
mouth.

With one hand—a glob of glue stuck to its sleeve—it extended a tambourine which it brandished menacingly (ah,
ah, ah).

> *Ol' man Faulkner make me sigh,*
> *Meek as Ella Cinder. Sigh?*
> *Black maid's sigh?*
> *Naw. Black maid's thighs was blackberry pies,*
> *'Sall it was,*
> *Coolin' on the winder.*

No mouth, and yet it spoke. The voice had lips and tongue
and breath and also a kind of history—each utterance was accompanied by a hissing, sparkling, ambient air, like that of an
old recording with a gold tooth. The voice was parody, the only
voice the figment owned, and as patented as wild rice.

> *Listen, Little Elbow Grease,*
> *Peckin' on your pica,*
> *Readin' Mod'n Library's*
> *Bad as breathin' ether.*
> *Ol' man Faulkner make you nod?*
> *(Drunk in his mimesis.)*
> *But don't you goddamn dare to try*
> *Amanuensis me!*

Reproach. This was Denial of Imagination. Copyright In-
fringement. Fear of Offending. Appropriation of Voice. Objection Sustained. Willful Misunderstanding. Preclusion. Scandal.
Minstrelsy. Ah, I knew exactly what it was. This was a New Orleans doll manufactured in wax, in 1922, by Madame Granger,
a Creole; this was Luther's doll, a figure of speech; my friend
Luther's phrase, the phrase that elicited nervous laughter from
me when I heard him use it in public: *You want I should pull
nigger out the bag?* (As he addressed a recalcitrant store clerk.)

I bent once more to my typewriter. I wrote: "Faulkner strained
to find the cadence of black patience and faith, creating his
own forgiveness in the person of Dilsey—Dilsey hovering over
her lost white charges."

> *Here he come, ol' skinny whey,*
> *Sobbin' in his 'kerchief—*
> *Whiney, piney, woe is me—*
> *"The South, the South," he constant say;*
> *He longin' for de dear ol' days.*
> *And you as bad as he is. Why?*
> *White child's Why?*
> *You confusin' grief with biscuits.*
>
> *—Why ain't there biscuits?—*
>
> *'Sall it was.*
> *Ain't enough I'm bought and sold,*
> *Ain't enough I'm weak and old,*
> *Still you goin' make me up—*

Say I smell like copper-gold;
Pour me in some nigger mold—
Some malaprop, some black tar soap,
Some hangin' rope, some 'bacca smoke—
You make me up, you make me up,
I don't exist, goddamn you.

'Cept
Some 'Mimah flapjack mix,
Some Cream o' Wheat steam
Risin' swift to ol' whey's
Quiv'rin' nostril.
Soon
I free the slaves that lick my pots
And bubble the swill that fill you—
Slave as plain as buttercup,
Slave as hot as forget-me-not,
Slave as shrill as daffodil—
Slaves wear them yella jackets.

"Faulkner strained to reproduce the cadence of Negro patience."

. . . Shoulda noticed the fire. Fiah. FIAH!

▪ ▪ ▪

As a young man, I was more a white liberal than I ever tried to put on black. For all that, I ended up a "minority," the beneficiary of affirmative action programs to redress black exclusion.

And, harder to say, my brown advantage became a kind of embarrassment. For I never had an adversarial relationship to American culture. I was never at war with the tongue.

Brown was no longer invisible by the time I got to college. In the white appraisal, brown skin became a coat of disadvantage, which was my advantage. Acknowledgment came at a price, then as now. (Three decades later, the price of being a published brown author is that one cannot be shelved near those one has loved. The price is segregation.)

I remain at best ambivalent about those Hispanic anthologies where I end up; about those anthologies where I end up the Hispanic; about shelves at the bookstore where I look for myself and find myself. The fact that my books are published at all is the result of the slaphappy strategy of the northern black Civil Rights movement.

Late in the 1960s, the university complied with segregation—the notion that each can only describe and understand her own, that education is a deeper solipsism, that pride is the point of education, that I would prefer to live among my kind at a separate theme-house dormitory; that I would prefer to eat with my kind at the exclusive cafeteria table where all conversation conforms to the implicit: *You Can't Know What I'm Feeling Unless You Are Me.*

In college, I revisited James Baldwin, seeking to forestall what I feared was the disintegration of my reading life, which had been an unquestioned faith in Signet Classics. My rereading of "Stranger in a Village" discovered a heavy hand. In the Swiss Alps, humorless *frauen* with crackled eyes go in and out their humorous houses, while on the twisting streets of the village, towheaded children point to Baldwin and shout after him *Neger! Neger!* ("From all available evidence no black man had ever set foot in this tiny Swiss village before I came.") So what is the point of the essay? It seemed to me Baldwin had traveled rather far to get himself pointed at; to arrange such an outlandish contrast; to describe himself as an outsider. And, too, the Alps seemed to represent Baldwin's obsession, an obsession that now seemed to stand between us.

This was not a generous assessment on my part, not a generous moment in my life. As a young reader, I would never have noticed or objected to Baldwin's preoccupation with White to the exclusion of all other kind. In the 1950s it would have seemed to me that a Negro writer was writing about the nation in which I was a part, regardless of whether my tribe was singled out for mention. But when the American university began to approve, then to enforce fracture, and when blood became the authority to speak, I felt myself rejected by black literature and felt myself rejecting black literature as "theirs."

Neither did I seek brown literature or any other kind. I sought Literature—the deathless impulse to explain and describe. I trusted white literature, because I was able to attribute universality to white literature, because it did not seem to be written for me.

William Makepeace Thackeray mocks my mother's complexion. And mine. My smell. My fingers. My hair. Cunning little savage. Little Jew. Little milkmaid. Little Cockney. Really, how can I laugh?

▪ ▪ ▪

The gym I attend in San Francisco is the whitest, the most expensive. Men and women read the *Wall Street Journal,* climb perpetual stairs pursued by grimacing voices.

Thump, thump, thump, thump. Stanzas, paragraphs, pages, hours, days, days, nights, days, *thump, thump, thump.*

Only Bach is as relentless, as monotonous, as cat's-cradled as hip-hop. Hip-hop is not music, in my estimation. (If music resolves.) Hip-hop does not progress, it revolves, replicates, sticks to the floor. It is not approximate emotion. It is approximate obsession. The "voice," the bard, the oracle, the messenger, the minister of propaganda intricately, saucily rhymes, chugs, foreshortens, sneers, insinuates, retreats. The voice betrays no emotion; has none; this is not rage, but cleverness. Too wise. Too sly. A dictatorship of rhyme. There is a message; the message is masonic; the conveyance too dense; deep as a trance. The voice is preoccupied and always in the present. It is the voice of schizophrenia. It is bad advice. It is the voice of battle—Beowolf, Edda, the madder psalms—the voice justifies endlessly. What is going to happen if you don't stop this! On and on and on. Slamming the table. It is the post-lude to music. Long after emotion has been flung from the bone, the beat remains. The beat plows through the rubble of music, turning under the broken arches of melody, stabbing about for rhyming shards—raising them, rubbing them together rhythmically—trying to ignite.

And what of the gym? They of the gym, we of the gym? Where is our allegiance? Is it to Queen Latifah or Gertrude

Himmelfarb? And if we of the gym are somehow, unconsciously, and in thrall to madder music, arming ourselves, it is for a battle against what?

▪ ▪ ▪

A few weeks ago, in the newspaper (another day in the multicultural nation), a small item: Riot in a Southern California high school. Hispanic students protest, then smash windows, because African-American students get four weeks for Black History month, whereas Hispanics get one. The more interesting protest would be for Hispanic students to demand to be included in Black History month. The more interesting remedy would be for Hispanic History week to include African history.

Hispanic students I meet on my speaking rounds complain of African-American students in their high schools or colleges. The complaint is that Black is preoccupied only with White; neither Black nor White will be dissuaded from a mutual vanity. I pretend not to understand the complaint. I play the adult. I answer the question with a question: *Why should they?* And then I turn around to write an op-ed about how the *New York Times* compiles a series on "race in America" that is preoccupied with Black and White.

I have not previously taken a part in the argument, the black-white argument, but I have listened to it with diminishing interest for forty years. It is like listening to a bad marriage through a thin partition, a civil war replete with violence, recrimination, mimicry, slamming doors.

■ ■ ■

I am not who I was. All the cells of my body have changed since I cradled Carl T. Rowan's book in my lap. I remain too much a cultural xenophobe, but also too convinced a mestizo to permit myself to claim any simple kinship with Black, with partition America. African Americans remain at the center of the moral imagination of America, which, I agree, is a very spooky place to be. Nobody else wants to be there, except by analogy. For it was there Africans were enslaved. It was there African Americans hung by their throats from trees. *Agnus Dei, qui tollis peccáta mundi, miserére nobis.* And what has emerged from the cocoon of African-American suffering, cut down from the tree, buried for half a century?

The boom. The boom. Superfly. Ropes of gold surround his resurrected neck. The glamour of the dead-eyed man.

I dislike to hear hip-hop at my gym. I am unfair. Do I object to the restriction of the form—as strict as a villanelle? Do I object to an outlaw romanticism? Do I object to the cadence of the pulpit given over to quixotism? Do I object to the immoral lyric chugging along a rhythm track, only concerned with finding the rhyme for muthafucka?

But then I admit I've never wanted to bite the tongue. I may have mastered the tongue, but I have never felt the need—or the love, incidentally—to invent a new one.

. . . Shoulda noticed the fiah!

Yes, I should have. But shut up for a minute. A few years ago, on a book tour, I found myself in a radio booth, the disappointed author (having just read a dismissive review of my second book in the *Washington Post*). I put the review aside. Played eager-to-please. *Thank you for having me.*

You didn't have me. And you didn't want me. Not that it matters; it was a whorish transaction, I knew that. The movie director Spike Lee had preceeded me onto the program in the previous hour, promoting his movie about Malcolm X. The African-American radio host suffered from time warp—*esprit d'escalier*—something he had said or left unsaid, I don't know.

So we remained shadows to each other, the interviewer and I. Departed Spike Lee was the only substance. At every break in the program, the interviewer would rise to pace the tiny studio, his body jerking with involuntary darns and double-damns—if only he'd thought to ask this or that.

He hadn't read my book. I watched the second hand of the clock on the wall. I didn't expect him to have read my book. I don't listen to his program.

I have been pondering what a black voice should sound like. A Baptist minister? An opera singer? A café artiste? Only to come to the conclusion a black voice should sound like parody? A brown voice should sound like rue?

No, that is not my conclusion. My conclusion is a measure of thankfulness: I cannot imagine myself a writer, I cannot imagine myself writing these words, without the example of African slaves stealing the English language, learning to read against the law, then transforming the English language into the American tongue, transforming me, rescuing me, with a coruscating nonchalance.

Come on now, you try it.

Chapter Two

IN THE BROWN STUDY

OR, AS A BROWN MAN, I THINK.

But do we really think that color colors thought? Sherlock Holmes occasionally retired into a "brown study"—a kind of moribund funk; I used to imagine a room with brown wallpaper. I think, too, of the process—the plunger method—by which coffee sometimes is brewed. The grounds commingle with water for a time and then are pressed to the bottom of the carafe by a disk or plunger. The liquid, cleared of sediment, is nevertheless colored; substantially coffee. (And coffee-colored has come to mean coffee-and-cream-colored; and coffee with the admixture of cream used to be called "blond." And vanilla has come to mean white, bland, even though vanilla extract, to the amazement of children, is brown as iodine and "vanilla-colored," as in Edith Sitwell's *where vanilla-coloured ladies ride* refers to Manila and to brown skin.) In the case of brown thought, though, I suppose experience becomes the pigment, the grounds, the *mise-en-scène,* the medium of refraction, the impeded passage of otherwise pure thought.

In a fluorescent-lit jury room, attached to a superior court in San Francisco, two jurors were unconvinced and unmoving. I was unconvinced because of the gold tooth two bank tellers had noticed and of which the defendant had none. The other juror was a man late in his twenties, rather preppy I thought on first meeting, who prefaced his remarks with, "As a black man I think . . ."

I have wondered, ever since, if that were possible. If I do have brown thoughts.

Not brown enough. I was once taken to task—rather, I was made an example of—by that woman from the *Threepenny Review* as the sort of writer, the callow, who parades his education. I use literary allusion as a way of showing off, proof that I have mastered a white idiom, but do not have the confidence of it; whereas the true threepenny intellectual assumes everybody knows everything, or doesn't, or can't, or shouldn't, or needn't, and there you are. Which makes me a sort of monkey-do.

Was I too eager to join the conversation? It is only now I realize there is no conversation. Allusion is bounded by Spell Check.

After such a long education most perceptions authentically "remind." And I'm not the only one. The orb Victoria held in her hand has passed to her brown children who, like Christ-children in old paintings, toy with the world a bit, and then, when no one is looking, pop it into their mouths. The only person I know for whom the novels of Trollope are urgent lives in India.

It is interesting, too, to wonder whether what is white about my thought is impersonation, minstrelsy. Is allusion inauthentic, Ms. Interlocutor, when it comes from a brown sensibility? My eyes are brown. *Cheeks of tan?*

Most bookstores have replaced disciplinary categories with racial or sexual identification. In either case I must be shelved Brown. The most important theme of my writing now is impurity. My mestizo boast: As a queer Catholic Indian Spaniard at home in a temperate Chinese city in a fading blond state in a post-Protestant nation, I live up to my sixteenth-century birth.

The future is brown, is my thesis; is as brown as the tarnished past. Brown may be as refreshing as green. We shall see. L.A., unreal city, is brown already, though it wasn't the other day I was there—it was rain-rinsed and as bright as a dark age. But on many days, the air turns fuscous from the scent glands of planes and from Lexus musk. The pavements, the palisades—all that jungly stuff one sees in the distance— are as brown as an oxidized print of a movie—brown as old Roman gardens or pennies in a fountain, brown as gurgled root beer, tobacco, monkey fur, catarrh.

We are accustomed, too, to think of antiquity as brown, browning. Darkening, as memory darkens; as the Dark Ages were dark. They weren't, of course, they were highly painted and rain-rinsed; we just don't remember clearly. I seem to remember the ceiling, how dark it was. How tall it seemed. The kitchen ceiling. And how frail we are! What used to be there?

A shoe store? A newsstand? I seem to remember it, right about here . . . a red spine, wasn't it? Have I felt that before? Or is this cancer?

At last, the white thought, the albin pincer—pain—an incipient absence, like a puddle of milk or the Milky Way. *The glacier knocks in the cupboard.* Why is cancer the white ghost? Why are ghosts white? And what year was that? Which play? Well, obviously it's Shakespeare. *Lear? Cymbeline? Golden lads and girls all must* . . . Death is black. Coffee may be black, but black is not descriptive of coffee. Coffee is not descriptive of death. Can one's life be brown? My eyes are brown, but my life? Youth is green and optimism; Gatsby believed in the green light.

Whereas there is brown at work in all the works of man. Time's passage is brown. Decomposition. Maggots. Foxing—the bookman's term—reddish brown; reynard. Manuscripts, however jewel-like, from dark ages, will darken. Venice will darken. Celluloid darkens, as if the lamp of the projector were insufficient sun. College blue books. Fugitive colors. My parents!

She doesn't remember me.

If we wish to antique an image, to make memory of it, we print it in sepia tones—sepia, an extract from the occluding ink of the octopus, of the cuttlefish; now an agent for kitsch. Whereas the colors, the iridescent Blakes at the Tate, are housed now in perpetual gloom, lest colors be lifted from the page by the cutpurse sun. The Kodachrome prints in your closet—those high-skied and hopeful summer days—are dimming their lights and the skies are lowering. Would we be astounded by the quality of light in 1922?

> *Unreal City,*
> *Under the brown fog of a winter dawn,*
> *A crowd flowed over London Bridge, so many,*
> *I had not thought death had undone so many.*

The prince had always liked his London, when it had come to him. And it had come to him that morning with a punctual, unembarrassed rap at the door, a lamp switched on in the sitting room, a trolley forced over the threshold, chiming its cups and its spoons. The valet, second floor, in alto Hindu cockney—and with a startled professionalism (I am browner than he)—proposed to draw back the drapes, damson velvet, thick as theater curtains.

Outside the hotel, several floors down, a crowd of blue- and green-haired teenagers kept a dawn vigil for a glimpse of their Fairie Queen. Indeed, as the valet fussed with the curtains, they recommenced their chant of: *Mah-don-ahh. Mah-don-ahh.* Madonna was in town and staying at this hotel. All day and all night, the approach or departure of any limousine elicited the tribute.

Mah-don-ahh was in town making a film about Eva Perón (both women familiar with the uses of peroxide. Not such a bad thing to know in the great brown world, *oi,* mate?).

I was in London because my book had just come out there. My book about Mexico. Not a weight on most British minds.

Did I ever tell you about my production of the *Tempest?* I

had been to the theater the previous evening. Not the *Tempest*, but the new Stoppard, and I watched with keener interest as the Asian in front of me leaned over to mouth little babas into the be-ringed ear of his Cockney hire. One such confidence actually formed a bubble. Which, in turn, reminded me of my production of the *Tempest*. (South Sea Bubble.) I would cast Maggie Smith as Miranda—wasted cheeks and bugging eyes—a buoyant Miss Haversham, sole valedictorian of her papa's creepy seminary. Caliban would be Johnny Depp. No fish scales, no seaweed, no webbed fingers, no claws, no vaudeville. No clothes. Does anybody know what I'm talking about? Ah, me. I am alone in my brown study. I can say anything I like. Nobody listens.

Will there be anything else, sir?

No, nothing else, thank you.

Brown people know there is nothing in the world—no recipe, no water, no city, no motive, no lace, no locution, no candle, no corpse that does not—I was going to say descend—that does not ascend to brown. Brown might be making.

My little Caliban book, as I say, bound in iguana hide, was about Mexico. With two newspapers under my arm, and balancing a cup of coffee, I went back to my bed. I found the Book section; I found the review. I knew it! I read first the reviewer's bio: a gay Colombian writer living in London.

What the book editor had done, dumb London book editor of the *Observer* had done—as Kansas City does and Manhattan does—is find my double or the closest he could find in greater London. It's a kind of dopplegänger theory of literary criticism and it's dishearteningly fashionable among the liberal-hearted. In our age of "diversity," the good and the liberal organize diversity. Find a rhyme for orange. If one is singular or outlandish by this theorem one can't be reviewed at all. Worse than that, if one is unlike, one will not be published. Publishers look for the next, rather than the first, which was accident. But the *Observer* wasn't even within bow-range. Their gay gaucho was clueless.

The liberal-hearted who run the newspapers and the university English departments and organize the bookstores have turned literature into well-meaning sociology. Thus do I get invited by the editor at some magazine to review your gay translation of a Colombian who has written a magical-realist novel. Trust me, there has been little magical realism in my life since my first trip to Disneyland.

That warm winter night in Tucson. My reading was scheduled for the six-thirty slot by the University of Arizona. A few hundred people showed up—old more than young; mostly brown. I liked my "them," in any case, for coming to listen, postponing their dinners. In the middle of one of my paragraphs, a young man stood to gather his papers, then retreated up the aisle, pushed open the door at the back of auditorium. In the trapezoid of lobby-light thus revealed, I could see a crowd was forming for the eight o'clock reading—a lesbian poet. Then the door closed, resealed the present; I continued to read, but wondered to myself: Why couldn't I get the lesbians for an hour? And the lesbian poet serenade my Mexican-American audience? Wouldn't that be truer to the point of literature?

Well, what's the difference? I do not see myself as a writer in the world's eye, much less a white writer, much less a Hispanic writer; much less "a writer" in the 92nd Street Y sense. I'd rather be Madonna. Really, I would.

The Frankfurt Book Fair has recently been overrun with Koreans and Indians who write in English (the best English novelist in the world is not British at all, but a Mahogany who lives in snowy Toronto and writes of Bombay). Inevitably, the pale conclusion is that brown writers move "between" cultures. I resist between; I prefer "among" or "because of." You keep the handicap. After all, it has taken several degrees of contusion to create a jaundice as pervasive as mine. It has taken a lifetime of compromises, the thinning of hair, the removal last year of a lesion from my scalp, the assurance of loneliness, the difficulty of prayer, an amused knowledge of five-star hotels—and death—and a persistence of childish embarrassments and ever more prosaic Roman Catholic hymns, to entertain a truly off-white thought. Here comes one now.

No, I guess not.

There's a certain amount of "so what?" that comes with middle age. But is that brown thought?

Thus did literary ambition shrivel in my heart, in a brown room in a creamy hotel in London, constructed as a nineteenth-century hospital and recently renovated to resemble a Victorian hotel that never existed, except in the minds of a Hispanic author from California and a blond movie star from Detroit.

▪ ▪ ▪

Eve's apple, or what was left of it, quickly browned.

Christ, a white doorway . . . was Bukowski's recollection of having taken a bite on the apple. When Eve looked again, she saw a brown crust had formed over the part where she had eaten and invited Adam's lip. It was then she threw the thing away from her. Thenceforward (the first Thenceforward), brown informed everything she touched.

Don't touch! Touch will brown the rose and the Acropolis, will spoil the butterfly's wing. (Creation mocks us with incipient brown.) The call of nature is brown, even in five-star hotels. The mud we make reminds us that we are:

> *In the sweat of thy face shalt thou eat bread, till thou return into the ground; for out of it wast thou taken . . .*

Toil is brown. Brueghel's peasants are brown, I remember noting in a Vienna museum.

In his book *Abroad*, Paul Fussell reminds us how, early in the twentieth century, the relative ease of modern travel and boredom allowed moneyed Americans and Europeans to extrude the traditional meaning of the laborer's brown and to make of it a glove of leisure. What the moon had been for early nineteenth-century romantics, the sun became for bored twentieth-century romantics. The brown desired by well-to-do Europeans was a new cure altogether: tan.

There is another fashionable brown. An untouchable brown. Certain shrewd ancient cities have evolved an aesthetic of decay, making the best of necessity. Decrepitude can seem to ennoble (or to create) whomever or whatever chic is placed in proximity—Anita Ekberg, Naomi Campbell. The tanned generation, a.k.a. the Lost Generation, gamboled through the ruins of the Belle Epoque. The *cardinali* of postwar drug culture—Paul Bowles, William Burroughs—found heaven in North Africa. It's a Catholic idea, actually—that the material world is redeemed; that time is continuous; that one can somehow be redeemed by the faith of an earlier age or a poorer class, if one lives within its shadow or its arrondissement or breathes its sigh. And lately fashion photographers, bored with Rome or the Acropolis, have ventured farther afield for the frisson of syncretism. Why not Calcutta? Why not the slums of Rio? Cairo? Mexico City? The attempt is for an unearned, casual brush with awe by enlisting untouchable extras. And if the model can be seen to move with idiot stridency through tragedy, then the model is invincible. Luxury is portrayed as protective. Or protected. Austere, somehow—"spiritual." Irony posing as asceticism or as worldly-wise.

One of the properties of awe is untouchability. *Silènzio,* the recorded voice booms through the Sistine Chapel at five- or ten-minute intervals. *Do not speak. Do not touch.* Even resurrected Christ—the White Doorway Himself—backed away from Mary Magdalene's dirty fingernails. Don't touch! I would have expected a Roman Catholic understanding of time to accommodate centuries of gaping mouths, respiration, prayer, burnt offerings—and reticence—offering the exemplum of a clouded ceiling to twentieth-century pilgrims. After all, we live in time. Our glimpse of the Eternal must be occluded by veils of time, of breath, of human understanding.

The human imagination has recently sustained a reversal.

One would have expected the pope, as the preeminent upholder of the natural order, to have expressed reservations about the cleaning of the Sistine ceiling. The pope, however, in a curiously puritanical moment, gave his blessing to a curator's blasphemy, which was underwritten by the Japanese fetish for cleanliness. The blasphemy was to imagine that restoring the ceiling might restore the Vatican's luster. The blasphemy was to imagine that time might be reversed. The blasphemy was to believe that time should be reversed.

The human imagination has recently sustained a reversal. We have cleaned the ceiling. Michelangelo's *Creation* and *Judgment,* the first and the last, and the pride of centuries—a vault over the imagination of the world—has been cleaned, has been restored; unhallowed; changed and called "original," though no one has any idea what that might mean. (What was the light of day in 1540?) Nile greens and rose-petal pinks, tangier oranges, and the martyred saints—what supernal beaver-shots. Well, we want them preserved, of course we do. And we are keen to see them as *they* saw them, the dead; as Michelangelo painted them. The very Tree of Knowledge has been restored, each leaf rinsed and all the fruit polished, the fruit and the sin repolished. Having seen, we also want them back the way they were.

We want what Eve wanted. . . . *Just curious.*

We had become accustomed to an averted eye, to seeing darkly, as old men see. It required many thousands of Q-Tips, many thousands of gallons of distilled water, which is to say, merely a couple of years, to wipe away the veil of tears, the glue from awakened eyes, to see born-again Adam touched by the less complicated hand of God. Now our distance from the representations, both alpha and omega, has been removed. And with it all credibility.

Blind John Milton—*brown all!*—dictating *Paradise Lost* to his aggrieved daughter in the dark, understood that what changes after Adam's sin is not creation, but our human relationship to creation. (We cannot be content, even on a warm winter day in L.A., but we must always carp about a white Christmas.)

Maybe Milton, in his preoccupation with the Fall, was more an ancient swarthy Catholic than a true, ready Protestant. (Protestantism was also an attempt to clean the ceiling.) Those famous religious refugees from Restoration England were (like Milton) Puritans who believed they had entered a green time and were elected by God to be new Adams, new Eves (as old John Milton could not, with the scabs of Europe grown over his eyes, and painted tropes of angels plaguing his memory—*brown all, brown all*).

Let us speak of desire as green. In the Roman church green is the vestment of Ordinary Time, a prosaic pathway. For American Puritans, green was extraordinary. They supposed themselves remade by their perilous journey to a new world they were determined to call green, proclaiming by that term their own refreshment. They had entered a garden ungardened and felt themselves free of history, free to reenact the drama of creation.

Green became the founding flag of America; and so it would remain for generations of puritans to come, whatever our religion or lack. American optimism—our sense of ourselves as

decent, naïve, primary people (compared to those violet, cynical races); our sense of ourselves as young, our sap rising, our
salad days always before us; our belief that the eastern shore
the Europeans "discovered" and the fruited plain beyond were,
after all, "virgin"—all this would follow from an original belief
in the efficacy of green.

Thus did the Dutch sailors in F. Scott Fitzgerald's *Great
Gatsby* spy the sheer cleft of an approaching "fresh green
breast." That same green breast is today the jaded tip of Long
Island, summer home to New Amsterdam investment bankers
and other rewarded visionaries who do not resemble their por-
traits. And the tragic hustler's ghost:

> *Gatsby believed in the green light, the orgiastic future that year
> by year recedes before us. It eluded us then, but that's no mat-
> ter—tomorrow we will run faster, stretch out our arms far-
> ther . . . And one fine morning—*

We—I write in the early months of the twenty-first century—
we are now persuaded by Marxist literary critics to goddamn
any green light; to hack away at any green motif. Someone off-
stage has suffered and no good can come of it. We are a college
of victims, we postmoderns; we are more disposed to notice
Fitzgerald's Dutch sailors were not alone upon the landscape
(we easily pick out chameleon Indians hidden among the green
tracery) than we are to wonder at the expanding, original iris:
How the Indians must have marveled at those flaxen-haired
Dutchmen.

Well, most likely the Indians were too terrified to morphologize or eroticize on the spot. What happens next? Watch, as the Indians did watch—with darker dread and puzzlement—what cargo these pale sailors unloaded. When: From below-deck emerged Africa in chains, the sun in thrall to the moon.

Thus, perceiving Europeans having only just arrived, the Indians already saw. Indians saw Original Sin. The dark ceiling. The stain spreading like oil spill. Rumor, too, must have spread like wildfire across the Americas—making green impossible from that moment, except as camouflage or tea.

Forgetting for the moment the journeys of others and the lateness of the hour; considering only the founding triad of our clandestine exhibit—Indian, European, African—we see (as well as the Founding Sin) the generation of the erotic motif of America. A brown complexity—complexity of narrative and of desire—can be foretold from the moment Dutch sailors and African slaves meet within the Indian eye.

I think I probably do. (Have brown thoughts.)

- *Chapter Three* -

THE PRINCE AND I

THE SCREEN AT PALO ALTO'S VARSITY THEATER WASN'T AS wide as it should have been. There were those 180-degree screens in San Jose where, if you sat in the first row, you would appreciate that a motion picture is a series of still frames. Even at the Varsity Theater, though, when T. E. Lawrence crossed the desert, the desert rendered Lawrence's person minuscule and his ambition gigantic. By force of will, T. E. Lawrence would claim the desert's name for himself. "Lawrence of Arabia" was a hero's name; an English schoolboy's imagination of the world as a playing field. Clive of India, Kitchener of Khartoum, Lawrence of Arabia.

Such is the potency of David Lean's film, I cannot conceive the man without the person of Peter O'Toole—white on white on white. His hair ostensibly bleached by the sun, his skin pale as sand; robes undulant as membranes of a sea anemone; his eyes madly blue.

The film's most memorable sequence begins when Lawrence dons the robes of Araby. His first impulse is the schoolboy's; he draws his pirate dagger. (The dagger becomes his looking glass.) His next impulse is to run, holding his diaphanous cape behind him to catch the wind—a delirious princess, a psalmist's bride.

Understand: I was a bespectacled dark-skinned English major at Stanford University when Peter O'Toole tripped gigantically, girlishly, across the screen of the Varsity Theater. Nevertheless, this vision of the hero as transvestite deeply pleased me and I privately issued a warrant—as a queen does to a marmalade company—to Lawrence of Arabia, for finding his eccentric place in the world of men.

Immediately I began reading *The Seven Pillars of Wisdom* wherein photographs revealed an author of only slightly less heroic cast than Mr. O'Toole, and much less mascara.

Who would approve an opposite tale? It was one thing for a hipless Englishman to play the swarthy pirate. The reverse would have been impossible to praise or to admire. Much less to film. No British director would film, in Cinemascope: *Rodriguez of the Reading Room!*

I was experimenting with impersonation. But why must I portray my ambition as impersonation? Not the Toffee who yearns to balance a cup and saucer on his knee, my ambition was to become conversant with American and British, mainly British, high literature—the best-known or best-said in a tongue I had determined to own.

I was experimenting with my body, trying to copy an ease

and heedless appetite I recognized in books as youth, but which my puzzling bookish mind could only emulate with dogged endurance. It was assumed, by the two or three people at Stanford who assumed anything at all about me, that I was in the library. I was not in the library. I went to the Stanford Stadium daily, to run around the track, then to run up and down the stadium steps. I was maddened by this impulse, this mimicry of my studies. I would go to the stadium two, then three times a day.

I was studying Puritanism and that, too, interested me; not least for its prohibition of impersonation.

At about this time, Malcolm X, an American puritan, discouraged African-American adolescents from hair straighteners and skin lighteners.

At about this time, ethnic studies departments were forming on some campuses. Such quorums would produce the great puritans of my age. The puritans would eventually form opinions about me, and I about them.

▪ ▪ ▪

Americans are in the habit of dressing the noun, "puritan," in the pejorative—puritan gray—meaning, in the main, sexual repression. I think America's deeper puritanical strain is evident in our fear of the stage, of all things theatrical. The wicked stage.

In the America of my youth, there was real life and there was theater (the red-and-gold disease, as Cocteau called it). Theater was a rival to Creation, to the business of earning money and raising children and watering the lawn. Our parents warned us against "big ideas." Big ideas were not good for us. The theater would give us big ideas that were inaccessible to us in our real lives.

In England, Puritans were famous for their objection to the confusion of the playhouse and to its seduction: The kettledrums and face powders and the actors lewdly strutting—boys playing women, rabble playing at kingship, rabble wearing the raiment of kings and speaking the sentences of kings, sentences no king could bear the weight of. Some historians believe that Puritans of Shakespeare's time were scandalized less by what transpired onstage than by the prostitutes and thieves, the sordid groundlings, who frequented the plays, conspired with kings.

"You are idle shallow things. I am not of your element," Malvolio shrieks to the pit, to the beggars and molls in the pit, even—it must be—at the actor playing himself. Malvolio is shamed by a tricked vanity, so, so, so, but to be judged by these! Noisemakers of Cheapside alleys, barefoot urchins splashing plague from puddles. And at court, too, he is mocked. Her Majesty laughs, therefore must Malvolio's original laugh at himself (Malvolio may have been a parody of Sir William Knollys).

Theatrics were an offshoot of liturgy—of the Mass, of the Passion and miracle plays and the lewd plays that preceded Lent. Puritans believed men were created to stand in pure relationship to God. Puritans ordained no intermediaries—no king or bishop or actor; no mother of God, no liturgy. Puritans had their day in England, in the seventeenth century. They severed the stalk of divine right. They dissolved all sham, dumb show, liturgy. Playhouses were shuttered and locked. And England kept a sober house.

But whirligig Time restores gaudy Aurora. After the Restoration, after the return of the anointed and the rouged, Puritans were once again persecuted in England. But before these great acts and their conclusions on the political stage of England, a small band of English Puritans set sail for America to pursue the freedom of an undivided relationship to God.

In early November, American grammar-school children used to be handed mimeographed drawings of Pilgrims to color. Pilgrims sailed over the horizon of November in sturdy brown ships, firing upon their antecedents—witches and pumpkins mostly. They came here to worship in their own way and to invent their isolation.

These Pilgrims were not the Canterbury kind, hiccuping and falling off their horses, devolving forever in their Prologue. The Canterbury pilgrims would be lucky to arrive before the twelfth grade. Grammar-school Pilgrims were an appealing, sober people with straight lines for mouths. They stood in the way of popish Christmas, but were themselves soon routed by snowflakes and candy canes and yellow Bethlehem stars.

Puritans composed a great American theme: One could become something new in America, something different from the cast-iron roles and faiths and the shackles that Europe imposed. But there was also something un-American about the Puritans' insistence upon a deathless identity once here. For America would turn out to be a land of inventors and self-inventors, a land of imposture. The theatrical possibilities of America would extend to blackface and feathers. Insofar as America would become an anti-Puritan country, Americans would dream of becoming other than they were. Insofar as America would remain a Puritan country, theatricality would meet the accusation of "inauthenticity." What is at stake in all this is the nature of authenticity, which is the Puritan dilemma.

From the first, there were Puritans and there were Indians and historical accidents—several parties converging upon the clearing in the woods. The exalted metaphor for that difference, for that convergence, was a turkey dinner. Indians came to the Thanksgiving feast dressed for Halloween. They had painted their faces and stuck feathers in their hair and they wore the skins of the animals of the forest. Birdcalls heralded their appearance in the clearing. Indians were theatricals impersonating Nature, portraying their place in Nature, which was also—and the Puritans saw it—their claim on the land.

And the Indians were royals; here was hierarchy and here was priesthood, even frippery. The costumes, the castes the Puritans had fled in England, America provided in savage parody. (As if the masques of court had pursued them in nightmare.)

The famous opposite tale of colonial America was that of Pocahontas. Her life reads as a Puritan parody; it certainly was an Anglican parody of Puritanism. She is a princess. We first hear of her cartwheeling down Main Street without any knickers on. (Her name meant "playful one.") As a child, Pocahontas saves the life of an Englishman. As an adult, she marries an Englishman, a different Englishman. She "goes native"; converts to her husband's church (the church the Puritans had fled); she takes the name of Rebecca. With her husband she travels back in time to London, toward her new innocence; assumes a title there. She is presented to Queen Anne. She is painted holding a plumed fan and with a garland of feathers upon the brim of her hat, a riding hat. She gives birth to a son and dies in England of the smallpox. She is laid to rest beneath an effigy, alongside the swift-flowing Thames. Her son later sails out to Virginia, marries there. Families in Virginia still claim some aristocracy as descendants of Pocahontas.

One hundred years after the death of Pocahontas, Joseph Addison, in a disquisition on London street signs, wonders at the Bell-Savage—a tavern sign—"which is the sign of a savage man standing by a bell. . . ." He conjectures the sign is a pictogram for the French, *belle-sauvage*. Might it not, as well, be a lost homage to the American princess?

One hundred years or so after Thanksgiving, the descendants of the first colonists would dress as Indians to portray themselves as authentic to their landscape, to portray the old country as having no claim on them, therefore. This was the Boston Tea Party.

Three hundred years after Thanksgiving a tribe of Indians at Stanford University would object to a theatrical Indian on the field of Stanford Stadium. Their puritan objection would be to the inauthenticity of the portrayal.

My interest is in this intersection—the intersection in America of the private theatrical with the public theatrical; the intersection of the closet and the meetinghouse; the impulse to play and the fear of play.

■ ■ ■

It is fall: I am sitting in the Stanford Stadium, in my year of T. E. Lawrence. I don't know if you remember those Saturdays in Palo Alto. The smell of peanuts and cigarettes, wet leaves. And smoke in the air. Remember how we cheered? Inauthentic to me, I confess. I wasn't interested in football. I wasn't cheered by the black- and white-skinned redskins—"Stanford Indians."

In those days many American high schools and colleges named their athletic teams "Indians," connoting physical prowess and, too, a renegade mythos. Tailgate parties, kegs of beer. And, too, an acrid poetic aroma of Indian summer that often accompanied the first contests of the school year.

But this day, the U.C.L.A. Bruins are overwhelming the Stanford Indians. I am wearing a costume I have copied from an illustration in *Esquire*—loafers, khakis, blue shirt, a red sweater draped over my shoulders. (Miles Standish.) At about this time, my younger sister decided to go to school in Paris. My mother wept and blamed me for all the "big ideas" I'd put in my sister's head. My sister was dry-eyed as she disappeared around the corner of the boarding gate; she never looked back. I had written a letter to her this morning. I couldn't wait for her to see *Lawrence of Arabia*; another big idea.

So many ironies played. I was, in those years, a most oblivious Indian. I did not think of myself as an Indian. Nor, incidentally, did Stanford. According to the logic and sympathy of my university, I was nothing more ancient than a "minority student," a new thing, freshly minted, a pilgrim. A minority, not because of my Indian face or Indian blood, but because I was related to Mexico. Were I, today, a student at Stanford, university bureaucrats would enlarge my disadvantage to describe it hemispherically—I would be Hispanic or Latino, not yet an Indian.

But there are Indians on campus during my time, oh yes. America is already far enough into the puritan revival we call "the sixties" so that some college and high school athletic teams are embarrassed to be named Indians. Angry American Indians at Stanford, impersonating angry African Americans, have already renamed themselves "Native Americans," thus disallowing the white irony of lost Columbus. (The Indians are learning to control parody, an American task.) We are already far enough into the sixties so that protests against the use of an Indian as an athletic mascot have been heard from the university's Native American theme house, where a tribe of undergraduates lives together, of a feather.

The Stanford Indian logo was a cartoon, an aspect of the Age of Disney. The Stanford Indian was a sort of troll. He had a big nose, red skin, pigtails, eyebrows expressive of peeve. The Stanford Indian was roughly a counterpart to Yosemite Sam; perhaps I misremember. He wasn't the Mohawk Gas sort of Indian, though, or the nickel sort. Certainly he was perceived as objectionable by Native American undergraduates. So the Stanford Indian had to go, and with him the bland, "flesh-colored" Pilgrim. The world would see them no more.

There was another Indian. His name was Timm Williams.

Williams, despite his name, was a "full-blooded" Yurok. Every Saturday home game during the football season, Timm Williams would take from his bedroom closet—I am making this up; I have no idea where Timm Williams kept his costume—would take from his bedroom closet a pair of buckskin britches, moccasins, a feathered war bonnet trimmed with fur. Thus attired, and somehow transported, Mr. Williams would step into the limelight of the Stanford Stadium as "Prince Lightfoot."

When Stanford was down, Prince Lightfoot menaced the opposing team; he put a "hex" on them. Whenever Stanford scored, a cannon fired. The Stanford band played. Blond cheerleaders—the "Stanford Dollies"—each wearing a headband with a single feather, rejoiced with a victory dance, whirled till they showed their underpants. Prince Lightfoot lifted his arms skyward in thanksgiving to the Great God Gridiron. *Shantih.*

■ ■ ■

All I know about Timm Williams's closet comes from a press release—an obituary—from the Stanford University News Service, 3-7-88, from which I quote:

> Williams was 27 and working for a steamship company in San Francisco when an Indian headdress that he had made caught the eye of a Stanford friend who wanted to wear it to the '51 Big Game.
>
> Williams said he wouldn't lend the headdress, but the friend

sent word back to Stanford boosters about him, and they promptly asked him to dance at a Big Game rally in San Francisco.

"I said I'd gladly do it, if they could get me tickets to the Big Game," [Williams] later recalled. The rally organizers agreed, and "Prince Lightfoot" began his reign.

Williams made his first trip to Stanford the next fall and performed at the bonfire in the sunken diamond. After his dance, a rally leader asked the crowd whether they wanted Prince Lightfoot as Stanford's official Indian. They cheered.

I privately derive an unsubstantiated inference or two: Timm Williams liked to dress up. He sought, through the theatrical invention of himself, to portray his true self to himself by playing the Indian publicly.

Subordinate conjecture: His spare time was spent making a feathered headdress. Intended to wear? Or as a spiritual exercise? It was not, I'm guessing, a Yurok headdress. In the photographs, it resembles a Plains Indian headdress.

Why did the friend send word back to Stanford boosters about him? (*You gotta see this guy?*)

Why two "m"s? Theatrical aspirations?

Why does one feel sure Timm Williams would have danced, even without tickets to the Big Game? His private impulse (making a headdress) wasn't private at all, as it turns out, but a revelation—for those with eyes to see. As one might leave a book out for a visitor to observe. *Oh that?* I think it more likely Timm Williams suggested to his friend he "send word back to the Stanford boosters."

What were the chances a young man who liked to dress up as an Indian prince would find his venue?

What were the chances history would find Timm Williams already suited up for the pageant of puritan dilemma—a public portrayal of his desire, a theatrical resolution to identity?

▪ ▪ ▪

Most every child reaches, at least once, for fantasies of violation or aspiration—mother's lipstick, daddy's jockstrap—the chance to become, not someone else, but someone approaching—true, recognized, breasted, distended.

Alas, remarked Mr. Ralph Waldo Emerson, "the voices which we hear (as children) in solitude . . . grow faint as we enter the world."

Do they?

College—the future—was represented to me in my adolescence by a pumpkin-colored settee in an illustration to the *Reader's Digest* condensed version of a novel called *Father to the Man*. A pumpkin-colored settee beneath a neo-Gothic window opened to a New England autumn—trees, steeple, cirrus cloud. Sprawled upon the settee was a lanky young man. From that one illustration I rented a future as furnished as memory—a future I would recognize when I saw it.

I have never found the room. The couch. The window. The pennants on the wall. Trophies on the mantelpiece. The piles of books and papers scattered about. The older man in a gray suit, regarding the younger . . . who is he? Is he the father?

One must be middle-aged to appreciate the longevity of

one's fantasy: the adult stands at the bathroom mirror, holding up his skin in anticipation of the time—I am emotionally certain it will come—when I shall be young again.

■ ■ ■

To speak now of loneliness, shadows that move at a tangent to sight, to reason, to the turn of the earth; imaginations, melodies, phrases, arrangements of color that torment for pleasing too much: Old people who live alone, we sometimes say of them that they become queer, by which we mean they succumb to private arrangements or explanations or expectations of things. They succumb to imaginations that are at some variance with what we, who move through traffic and collect pay, call the real world.

Edith Sitwell defined eccentricity, the private theatrical, thus: "Any dumb but pregnant comment on life, any criticism of the world's arrangement, if expressed by only one gesture, and that of sufficient contortion, becomes eccentricity."

When it breaks the surface of the water: A fat, shy, brown boy in a swimming pool twirls underwater and then breaks through the surface, covered with gems and diamonds. And his hair is like seaweed or like a seal's cap; he is very beautiful. Ganymede or Hephaestion. *How did you learn such grace, so young a boy?*

I cannot know anyone's solitude. I am content to stand in relation to Timm Williams, as to someone who sought a limelight in which to portray himself. Of the private theatrical that propelled him thence I can say nothing. And yet that is the theme that interests me. That is the theme of Prince Lightfoot's career and theatrical martyrdom. Of the bathroom mirror as the imagination of a public life, I am prepared to speak. I substitute my own longing, my own solitude, which had nothing to do with the compulsion to make or to wear an Indian costume.

I used to study the theater ads in the Sunday *New York Times*. I absorbed the style of them, the ads; the style of New York in the fifties. Theater posters of my youth were drawn. This was an aspect of technology. The only feasible reproductions were drawn images transferred onto plates. Photographs could not at that time be so easily or so cheaply reproduced.

I would isolate one poster as emblematic of what I most liked, a poster by Morrow—if I said the ubiquitous Morrow, you would not know what I was talking about. But you would recognize the poster for *Auntie Mame*. The play. The image seems to have been sketched with a mascara brush and a tube of lipstick.

On the poster, the glitter of rhinestones and the jangle of bracelets are suggested by confetti jots of colored pencil. There is always a certain weightlessness and a certain whoopie to the best theater posters. And the best find new ways to convey the oldest theatrical bleat:

Darling!

The eponymous possibility, too, is irresistible. Someone "as" or someone "in." An irrational hope within the human psyche is the hope of finding one's role, a role that will represent one— the Marschallin, Hamlet, Margo Channing—as opposed to one's puritan authenticity. The role is the immortal part; we but transient spirits.

*Richard Rodriguez in "The Reading Room." Timm Williams
as "Prince Lightfoot."*

At curtain: The young man enters through a door, stage
right. He carries with him a valise, an overcoat, an Indian
headdress. The setting is a sitting room in a boardinghouse
near a New England college campus. It is afternoon. The room
is empty, except for a large Victorian settee, pumpkin-colored,
soiled, torn, too large to evacuate—which faces away from
large double windows recessed in a slanting wall. This is obviously an attic room. The windows are closed. Empty bookcases
line one wall, stage left. There are unfaded patches on the wall
where pictures have been removed. There is an empty coatrack upstage. The young man surveys the room, sets down his
valise in front of the settee, places his overcoat upon the valise.
He notices the coatrack, crosses, hangs the Indian headdress
upon it. He peeks through a door, stage left. He walks behind
the settee to open the double window . . .

. . . Emotion stirs within the orchestra pit, which is a caul-
dron of muddle, attempting to clarify. Emotion laps at the
apron of the stage throughout the scene and will eventually
flood the narrative, for this is a musical.

It is not the song per se that we lack in our real lives. There
are plenty of songs in the world. It is the song-within-narrative
that we lack, of which there are many types. There are choruses, duets, trios. There are patter songs, simple ditties. It is
the promise of a song at the right moment that we lack; the
transfiguring song. What most matters is the soliloquy.

The soliloquy is an occasion for explanation. For putting one's
case before oneself in private (privacy is represented by direct

address to the audience). Theatrical soliloquy achieves what private deliberation attempts, what prayer attempts, yearns for, but can never seem to accomplish in life. I suppose the completing reciprocation would be applause—some immediate response, miracle, or show of grace (as represented by confetti on the poster).

Within the theater, there is the pathetic veracity of the orchestra pit. Loneliness is a chord or a descending scale. Anger is a drum. Danger a trombone, as Carmen turns over the fated card. Epiphany is ethereal—a zither, a harp, triangle; something such.

"One" is the auditor, but also someone else: It is that your mother or father or your brother is in the kitchen, wondering why you find this stuff so compelling. They end up knowing the songs—how could they not? They are blasted with them, day and night. But they assign no narrative power to the songs, as you do. Occasionally, transparently, to please you, they will make a request. But you can't just play that song in isolation. They are so stupid. You must earn it; work up to it. To them, these are just songs. Inexplicable songs, screechy, brassy, overheated songs; unlovely voices.

The Original Cast Album was an imprimatur of sorts, to certify "this really happened," nightly, before an audience of 900 people. Gertrude Lawrence actually performed the role, spoke the lines, moved in costume through the narrative of a life onstage. Thus, a kind of reality extends from the rapt imagination of the teenager on his couch, to the recording studio on West Fifty-fourth Street, to the stage of the St. James Theater, to the mind, the life, the loneliness, the disappointment of the poet, the lyricist, sitting at a table—some arrangement of lamplight and ashtray and zither—inventing a posthumous adolescence, inventing a luminous future.

The young man throws open the double windows—his gesture elicits a tingle from the pit, a sustained anticipatory threshold through which passes first the drum, then the rocking harmonium of bass and oboe—the vamp—but as yet unfreighted with melody. The young man surveys the quad below, turns, walks around the settee; a cymbal beat joins the drum; he tests the cushions, sits, then reclines; abruptly stands, walks to the coatrack, lifts down the headdress, places it on his head; returns to the settee, sits cross-legged, "Indian-wise," folds his arms, sings:

> *When I think of Tom*
> *I think about a night*
> *When the earth smelled of summer*
> *And the sky was streaked with white,*
> *And the soft mist of England*
> *Was sleeping on a hill . . .*

In four stanzas, three choruses, he will tell you everything about his life so far and what his hopes are and where he's bound and what he has left behind. He will reveal an inner life that separates him from the narrative. Sings:

> *I remember this,*
> *And I always will . . .*

There are new lovers now on the same silent hill,
Looking on the same blue sea,
And I know Tom and I are a part of them all,
And they're all a part of Tom and me.

Her voice will conceal with deportment that she is too old for the part by a decade or so; why she uses so much eyeliner. Gertrude Lawrence had a tendency to go flat and she had to fight to get her songs transposed down a third. All the disappointments of her life—and yours—converge on the shore of this reverie. The song laps at the hem of her gown. She can see fragments of her coming life stored in the wings, flotsam beginning to lift on the tide of music—hatboxes, a writing desk, a deathbed. She turns to face the audience; she opens her eyes preternaturally wide to the spotlights focused upon her. Then, from the diaphragm, the first step onto air:

Hello, young lovers, whoever you are,
I hope your troubles are few . . .

You turn up the volume so they can hear it in the kitchen—this part, where the orchestra seems to breathe like a field in summer. You know very well what a field in summer sounds like, but you prefer this redeemed version. So that, henceforward, as you walk a country road, the field will become this, an orchestra! Or this part, the finaletto to act one, the pompous kettledrum amuses; the orchestra becomes an aural equivalent of a curtain's plunge.

But they never do hear it. Life intervenes. The phone rings.

A thought springs from their inattentive heads. Or the vegetables come to a boil. The coffee grounds which have sat all morning must at this moment be emptied into the pail with that *thump, thump, thump.* Someone flushes a toilet. Or someone turns on the tap. The spell you are broadcasting is so fragile it can be drowned by a kitchen tap.

James Woods, in a recent essay, construes soliloquy in the theater as "blocked conversation." In my youth the musical comedy soliloquy was the perfect vehicle for blocked homosexual emotion—self-effacing epiphanies, reconciliations to disappointment. Vows. Examinations of conscience, rather as the church taught. The song about how much I love him but he'll never know it.

And he never did.

I once had a teacher who wrote in a letter, "Tell me the truth, even if you have to dissemble." Dissembling was the specialty of Broadway musicals. The storylines were scrupulously heterosexual. What could I have heard in them that made me think they explained me? It was this: The innocent characters were so wonderfully compromised by the actors who played them; by the writers and musicians who created them. The scar tissue on voices. The makeup on faces. Youth! The wicked stage! The jaded legend refreshed the innocence of my youth.

Musical comedy songs were more real than my life because they were articulate and because they had ligaments of narrative attached to them. For today's young queers and lonelys, these songs must seem quaint and campy and not useful. But they were never campy for me—for us?—they only became camp in the attempt to share them without embarrassment. It became necessary to distance ourselves from memories of a solitude so comic, perhaps, and yet so rich and so holy—huge balloons of rhyming thought hung in the air, lapidary, efficacious, memorable—and the world (represented by the narrative) stopped.

The emotion of these songs is both retroactive and proactive. Once you have fit your own emotion to these words, the words will forever after find your emotion; will, at some unforeseen time, explain your emotion to you, unbidden.

And the narrative resumes.

▪ ▪ ▪

Many years later, long after I leave Stanford, I will be pursued in print by some puritan professor there for exhibitions of ethnic self-hatred in my writing. Yes, as a child, I dragged a razor blade against the skin of my forearm to see if I could get the brown out. I couldn't. A clandestine experiment. Just checking. Did I hate my brown skin? No. Would I rather have been white? I would rather have been Jeff Chandler. Jeff Chandler would rather have been Lauren Bacall, according to Esther Williams's autobiography.

And yet I remain as much a puritan as any American. I remember, as a boy, being perplexed by a real-estate agent (a neighbor) wearing a red fez and riding a miniature motorcycle in the Shriners' parade.

I went to a performance of *Death of a Salesman* in New York last year. I had a box seat very near the stage, at a raised and acute angle. I could see into the wings. The wonderful actress who played the wife became so emotionally engaged in the final scene, the graveyard scene, she could not come out of her grief at the end of the play. She had to be helped to her bows by the other actors. This interested me.

I have noticed, during speaking engagements, that I sometimes feel a freedom to weep, to assume voices, to carry on in public, to channel in shameless ways. This freedom alarmed me the first time I entered it, because I was not sure how to get "out" or back to myself, to straighten myself, as a puritan must.

I only mean to suggest we live in a nation whose every other impulse is theatrical, but whose every other impulse is to insist upon "authenticity."

▪ ▪ ▪

In his book *Playing Indian,* Philip J. DeLoria, a Native American academic, describes the long habit of white Americans to undress themselves as Indians, from Boy Scouts to Natty Bumpo, the Improved Society of Red Men, all the way back to the Boston Tea Party.

It has been a satisfaction to American boys to play Indian. The impersonation is a license to wildness. Off with the shoes! Off with the shirt! Pee in the bushes; no one can see. Throw rocks at the magpies. No more teachers, no more books. Scalp the girls, make them cry.

Westward expansion was dependent upon Indian ways and Indian guides; frontier bilingualism. Early white settlers in America had to learn Indian ways for survival. But the white man took his instruction in civilization as initiation into savagery. As western migration continued, the white man fully supplanted the Indian upon the landscape. By the nineteenth century, Europeans began to regard all Americans as savage, as having taken on the savagery of the landscape. For the most part, Americans were gratified by this designation.

I have in my possession an old book with an illustration that probably dates from sometime between the wars. It is a cartoon in two panels, attributed to John T. McCutcheon of the *Chicago Tribune*. In the first panel, an old man, sitting on a log, Whitmanesque—slouch hat, long white beard, pipe—is spinning a yarn for a little boy, perhaps his grandson. The two regard an autumn field. Shocks of corn recede into the distance. Colored autumn leaves on the tree against which they rest. They rest, having raked leaves—the old man holds a rake and there is a pile of burning leaves in the foreground. There is mist upon the distance of the field and the sun will shortly go down.

In the second panel, we see what the old man has conjured for the boy. It is night. The sun has become a harvest moon. The burning leaves have become a campfire. The shocks of corn are teepees amongst which ghostly Indians dance a ghostly dance. The cartoon is titled "Injun Summer."

I describe this particular drawing only because it so exactly depicts Indians as having become figments of white imagination; depicts whites as keepers of the legend. One notices in American poetry, in Longfellow and in Whittier, how secret or divulged knowledge of the landscape passes from the Indian boy to the barefoot boy, the delightful new savage:

. . . How the beavers built their lodges
Where the squirrels hid their acorns . . . ("Hiawatha")

How the tortoise bears his shell,
How the woodchuck digs his cell . . . ("Barefoot Boy")

Many Americans, black as well as white, claim Indian blood. The Indian was curiously free, within the white rule, to marry both the white and the black. "I am the only Negro in the United States whose grandfather on the mother's side was *not* an Indian chief," wrote Zora Neale Hurston.

Half-breed, in American English, when it referred to Indian-white mixture did not describe an irredeemable contaminant state, but rather a streak of wildness—*You bad half-breed girl!* The Indian's wildness could be tamed by dilution, by further breeding with Europe. Thomas Jefferson made a curious distinction between black and Indian. Jefferson wished for the integration of Indians into white society; felt that America would be ennobled by that consanguinity. Even while he bedded his slave, Jefferson expressed no similar public wish for a black-white society.

Americans speak of wildness, too, as a taste in game—the flavor of grass and insects, the taste of landscape—but also as a fundamental and profound incapacity for trust or allegiance. In my childhood, wild game was often marinated in cow's milk—the symbol of American domesticity—in order to "soak the wildness out of it."

▪ ▪ ▪

And how to explain the different place accorded the Indian and the African in the white imagination? The Indian refuses to accomplish the European's will on the land (it is his religion he will not have violated). It becomes the African slave's task to till the soil, to plant and to reap. By sowing, the African enters into American history. However unwillingly, he consorts with Europeans. The African becomes the enslaved proxy in the white domination of Nature. From this arrangement, the White assumes that the African wants to become like his master (because he already is like his master, he is doing his master's will).

From this arrangement, the African learns parody, first in earnest, for self-preservation, then in loathing.

From this arrangement, the white man learns parody, first in loathing, then in earnest.

From this point in American history, the African takes over the narrative; the Indian remains the odd man out, sticks to his reserve, embitters himself, while the white man makes him up. The Indian, as much a puritan as any Puritan, as regards identity, never gets a handle on parody or, indeed, on self-parody.

■ ■ ■

After the Civil War, white Southerners felt themselves bereft. Their way of life was judged by their victors to have been an abomination. After black emancipation, whites, in their loneliness, invented happy Negroes, a happy Babylon of singing and dancing. They invented the American musical. These were the minstrel shows.

It is conventional in America now to view the minstrel shows as only mockery—blackened faces and transvestism (white men also played black women in minstrel shows). The greater mockery was in daring to attribute nostalgia for captivity to black folk. The nostalgia was entirely a white invention, all that mammy stuff, uncle stuff; familial parody. The most famous purveyor of white "ethiopian airs," as minstrel songs were called, was Stephen Foster. Most of his songs were written in Pennsylvania; Foster hadn't much knowledge of the South and was forever consulting gazetteers for the names of rivers. Foster's songs masqueraded as songs overheard on an old plantation. But they were pathetic love songs sung by white people to black people in the guise of mockery.

Black people, of course, have steadfastly refused all pathetic suits. *I never loved you. You are deluded.*

By the 1920s, Al Jolson broke the immigrant son's silence—and he did so in blackface. Here again we gather the puritan theme of America to the parodist's theme: Jolson's father was a cantor in a synagogue who disapproved of theater-singing as inappropriate to a Jew. The only way for a young Jewish man to sing from his heart on a stage, to be authentic to his private yearning, was to do so in blackface—a protective masquerade, also an emulation of the supposed freedom of black people.

Shortly after Al Jolson broke the sound barrier, Edgar Rice Burroughs's creation of Tarzan—in print, comics, and later on the screen—moved many American boys toward the game of naked Africans or "natives." Tarzan is not an African, but a peer of the realm, an accidental Indian, an inauthentic savage, an innate gentleman, a natural puritan, an ecologist. (It is a very confusing parable.) But the main point taken by American boys is that, while Tarzan is white, he finds his meaning in darkest Africa.

Only decades after Jolson and Tarzan, Norman Mailer wrote an intriguing essay, "The White Negro," which comes very close to telling the truth about greasepaint and footlights and finding the company of one's desire. The white hipster went uptown, as to wilderness, to listen to jazz in the forbidden playhouse. A generation later, if white Americans were still not willing to admit to an envy of blacks, they were at least willing to applaud Elvis Presley for daring to play B. B. King. Whites were putting on black culture and calling it their own.

Soon, an unrepentant charmer named Cassius Clay introduced a new game to the American playground: black braggadocio. *I'm the greatest!* Clay spoke in jingle rhymes and he was all that he said he was, an authentic American hero. Even after Cassius Clay renamed himself Muhammad Ali, his espousal of Islam—the puritan impulse—did not seem at odds with the playfulness of his self-promotion or his occupation, which was of the playhouse.

In Ali, did America finally have an integrated, playful puritan? Perhaps. But puritanism not only weathered the dawning era of blackface (everyone in the sixties wanted to claim the black analogy), puritanism defined the era: wire-rimmed glasses, unshaved legs, bra burnings, campus witch trials, the rejection of "role-playing" and the rejection of authority, tradition—the university president as British sovereign. And don't forget the smugness and sourness; the humorlessness, literalness, that characterized the Native American at a school like Stanford, for example, or the Chicano or the black—the insistence on delineating what was offensive, or, better, oppressive or, better, inauthentic.

At a time when the Stanford Dollies were beginning to be instructed in sexual victimization, at a time when white football players were slapping hands in the end zone in imitation of Cab Calloway, a Yurok Indian named Timm Williams would be banned from playing the role of Indian at Stanford. That's the puritan truth. And reasons for the ban were the purest puritan: Native American students on the Stanford campus, and Native Americans who were not of the campus, objected to the heroic portrayal of the Indian as demeaning to them. A rejection of pageantry as inauthentic. I quote from a Stanford University News Service release (10-11-79):

> The term Indians was first used by sportswriters, then adopted by students before [the] Big Game in 1930. It was officially dropped following quiet discussions with Native American students in 1972, when the student senate also voted against its continued use.
>
> In 1972 [Stanford President] Lyman told alumni his talks with American Indian students at Stanford had indicated that "if there is any effect whatever from [use of] the heroic Indian symbol, it is to romanticize and perpetuate an illusion about the American Indian.
>
> "The American Indian students don't want today's problems to

be concealed in what they regard as always a somewhat com-
mercialized and always somewhat fake representation even of
the Indian tradition," Lyman continued.

"They talk about religious dances [at sports events] being pro-
fane, they talk about the impact it has upon them to see pseudo-
Indian motifs worked into pompon girls' costumes, and so on."

(Nor would Timm Williams lend his headdress—as if that
were some profanation of the role.)

In 1971, my sister returned from Paris. She had found that her
look—*la mexicaine*—played very well in Paris and she played
Paris very well. She returned with long Audrey Hepburn coats
and short, very short, skirts. And her hair, always plentiful and
lustrous, was wildly teased and tossed. She went to Harvard
Business School, where she evolved a playful theory of haute
couture as theatrical parody of the mundane. She filled my
head with big ideas. She established in my mind that the only
point to becoming an intellectual was to become a public intellectual. She established in my mind that a public intellectual
should be glamorous: *Stop dressing like a graduate student.*
Then she married a judge and gave birth to theatrical children.

In 1972, I went to London to study. I did become, for a time,
Rodriguez of the Reading Room. I balanced many a teacup on
my knee. I met people. I knew people. Not well. Not well at
all. I went to plays, that was my lonely passion and my parish.
On a rainy night in March, a Thursday night, I would take
up my umbrella and walk out to watch Gielgud illuminate a
half-empty theater. I saw everything and everyone. I sat in the

cheap seats, young enough to hear every word of the tenuous conversation of the time—they were broken conversations. Blocked. If Gielgud dried up, it didn't matter, for the conversation was characterized by stammer. The china was chipped, the carpet frayed, and the stage lighting pale—"an afternoon in early spring." A generation was flickering, dying. I was growing younger, heedless.

▪ ▪ ▪

In October 1979, at fifty-six years of age, Prince Lightfoot attempted a Stanford comeback, in gangster fashion, "accompanied by several men wearing T-shirts," and of a "threatening demeanor" (*Stanford Daily*, 10-8-79, and ff.):

> Timm Williams returned to the Farm Saturday, receiving a mixed response of cheers and boos from the seventy thousand fans. . . . Williams was appearing as . . . Chief Lightfoot for the first time in seven years. There are conflicting reports on how Williams, who had no pass, was allowed on the field. . . . He waved to the crowd and then slowly circled the track, accompanied by men who acted as cheerleaders by waving their arms to solicit applause.
>
> As he paraded in front of the student section . . . Williams received both boos and cheers.
>
> Although band members said they had been told to "just ignore" Williams, they included a native American fanfare in their post-game show. Williams began dancing, but stopped when persons in the stand began throwing ice and trash.

▪ ▪ ▪

The final theatrical question in America concerns old age (beginning with middle age): how to behave "appropriately," dress appropriately, assume a role that feels inauthentic and for which one is never emotionally prepared (one has seen others take the role so admirably). Remember, the mermaid no longer sings for you, old sport, nor does the wolf whistle. *Oh, what the hell. That will have to do. Nobody's going to be looking at me anyway.*

Two years ago, I am late for a dinner in London. Ten-thirty and the after-theater crowd is barking happily, yelping yuppily throughout this bright, meaty restaurant. *Ooops.* My party has arrived and is already seated. *Yes, I see them. Pardon me. Yes, yes, wavey, wavey. I'm coming.*

Suddenly over a shoulder, I catch a glimpse of him. A voice and a glow from his table announce his presence, as do busers who hover. His arm is draped around the back of a woman in gray. He turns, a three-quarter profile, and as he turns, his eyes catch mine. They are still madly blue.

On June 15, 1816, William Hazlitt addressed readers of the *London Examiner* concerning the rumored return to the stage of the famous Mrs. Siddons:

> Players should be immortal, if their own wishes or ours should make them so; but they are not. They not only die like other people, but like other people, they cease to be young and are no longer themselves, even while living. Their health, strength, beauty, voice, fail them; nor can they, without these advantages,

perform the same feats, or command the same applause that they did when possessed of them. It is a common lot: Players are only *not* exempt from it.

T. E. Lawrence portrayed himself heedlessly—went native—betrayed his tribe, pursued a private sense of authenticity. The English could never see it. What did he think he was doing, traipsing around dressed like that, so chummy with the Toffees? *The bugger.*

But the Arabs saw. If an Arabian could be thus portrayed, then there must be, then there would be an Arabia.

Before he took the role of Lawrence, Peter O'Toole consented to a producer's suggestion he change his nose. Whatever his Irish nose had been was replaced by an English nose, which, of course, he kept; which is how we recognize him—for Lawrence portrayed him authentically.

■   ■   ■

When Prince Lightfoot stepped upon the field of Stanford Stadium to thunderous applause he was the distillation of an Indian, the Mohawk gas, the nickel sort, the Edward Curtis, the Burt Lancaster. His face painted, his arms fringed, his breastplate rattling, he drew majesty; tom-toms intoned the mystery of his glance. But the puritan Indians of Stanford would not approve, in their Monday hearts, a musical-comedy Indian. Puritans distrust the efficacy of art.

Harry Demar "Timm" Williams, [who] personified Stanford's Indian mascot from 1951 until it was abolished in 1972, died Sunday, March 6th, when his compact car was hit broadside at an intersection in Crescent City, Calif. He was 64.

. . . His last official appearance as the Indian was at the 1972 Rose Bowl, where he was carried off the field triumphantly . . . [Stanford University News Service 3-7-88].

Do not for a moment, darling, imagine I propose Timm Williams's story as a sad story. His is a triumphant story. And if I seem to have fashioned from its shadow, from the privacy he wore, from all I cannot know, a parable for my own life, do not, for a moment, think you know what an Indian is. You are idle, shallow creatures. And we are not of your element.

▪ ▪ ▪

Someone once described to me seeing a matinee of *The King and I* in New York. At the intermission, outside the theater, as my informant was pacing around with his *Playbill* scrolled in his hand, he heard a sound like sweeping, like pavement being swept. He glanced down into the dark stairwell at the side of the theater and there he saw the star of the play, Gertrude Lawrence, in her second-act ball gown (dragging upon the pavement)—the most famous ball gown in theatrical history; the ball gown that will shortly be whipped through the real air of the stage during the "Shall We Dance?" polka, a moment of theater so purely accidental, so rehearsed, so wonderful that an encore is now standard in any production.

Gertrude Lawrence is wearing her Titian-colored wig. A diamond bracelet glitters upon her wrist. She is smoking as she paces back and forth. Within three months she will be dead. She will be buried in this ball gown. From which we can take it—if we take nothing else—that roles are to be taken seriously, not only by those of us who listen in the dark, but also by those transfigured personalities who move, for a time, in the light.

- *Chapter Four* -

POOR RICHARD

THERE WAS NOTHING HEROIC ABOUT THE FIGURE OF BENJAMIN Franklin, bespectacled, portly, subtle, radical, dangerous.

In grammar school—and as new to American history as to the American tongue—I nevertheless puzzled through several junior biographies of Franklin because young Ben's ambition magnified my own. I kept lists in those years of the books I read. I recognized the yearning to escape the limits of family— "a strong inclination for the sea"—as well as some more vertical yearning: a boy becomes a man by gaining wisdom; each book a rung therefore; each rung a classical tag. I weighed the shame of the sordid candle shop where Franklin was forced to work for his father against the optimism of old New England. Ben greeted each new-minted morning with the self-improving question: *What good shall I do this day?*

The only other federal figure who interested me as much as

81

Benjamin Franklin was Richard Milhous Nixon. I did not admire Nixon, his name a negation. I recognized him. The part of my formation that was not tutored by Franklin—Franklin recommending the society of right-minded men—was fascinated by Nixon, his knock-kneed stealth.

Because of Franklin, I went in my black suit to improving lectures where I took notes. One night an address by Eleanor Roosevelt. Another week a diplomat in sunglasses from New Delhi. I purchased tickets to touring Broadway plays—they used to call them "bus and truck companies," the kind that came to Sacramento—ennobling plays like A *Man for All Seasons* and *Sunrise at Campobello*. I loved them because they were improving. My black suit was the uniform of self-improvement, of the seminarian, the apprentice, the Machiavel. I wore mine from eighth grade to college—taken in, let down. My black suit made me invisible and that was its point. Respectably shabby, and that was its point. I could go to the opera. I could go to New York.

But I would never wear the black suit as patrician George Washington wore a black suit, or John Kennedy for that matter. I wore a black suit as Nixon wore a black suit. As Malcolm X wore his. It was the putting on of sweat rings and dried lips and bright eyes, the black suit. Unease, yes, but also optimism. Nothing so dries out a young man's skin as the black suit. It never fits. Mine didn't. It wasn't supposed to fit, the kind of suit I had, the acolyte's suit. It was appropriate. There is nothing so attractive to the world as an ardent young man in an ill-fitting suit. Whereas a young man in a well-fitting suit has joined . . . something.

Because of Nixon, on Monday nights I'd tell my parents I was going to Boy Scout meetings, and I went instead, alone and in my Boy Scout uniform, to the smoke-filled, cigar-scented pro wrestling matches at the Memorial Auditorium. There I joined Okie women in flannel shirts and teenaged Mexican farmworkers, and several hundred other spectators who knew the game in America was rigged against them.

In the light of day, at my Catholic high school, it was Kennedy versus Nixon. It was Kennedy, of course. Just so, to earn extra credit (a kind of Nixonian stealth), and to attract the notice of my English teacher (another), I wrote a book report on *Profiles in Courage*, which must be a very good book because it won a Pulitzer Prize. The book did not interest me.

I admired a darker grain. Reading Nixon was a private pleasure whereby I sought another league. I was first at my public library to check out *Six Crises*. I read with shrill pleasure Nixon's recollection of the call to boyish ambition: "Only one train a day went through the town of Yorba Linda (population then of less than 300) and hearing its whistle as it slowed down at the crossing never failed to start me to daydreaming about the places I would visit when I grew up."

In those years, I hadn't learned to cover my ambition by feigning detachment. At an all-boys' high school, naked ambition was certainly acceptable on the playing field, where players could dote with unironic concentration on "Coach"—Coach's Adam's apple, Coach's gold fillings, Coach's wedding ring, the tassel of corn silk at Coach's throat; all the mysteries. Fawning ambition so plainly expressed in the classroom was quite another matter. It wasn't that I got A's; other boys got A's. It was that I wanted my A's so badly and sought them so blatantly— that's what everyone saw.

Nixon: "I won my share of scholarships, and of speaking and debating prizes in school, not because I was smarter but because I worked longer and harder than some of my more gifted colleagues."

Courtiers of the Italian Renaissance extolled a locution of insouciance they named *sprezzatura,* which translates to nonchalance. The young Florentine was schooled to study the art of the courtier so well, so habitually, as to transform his own demeanor to an artless grace. There was to be no seam to seeming; no nurture to naturalness. Such an idea should repel Americans. American myth celebrates becoming—the awkward journey of effort and pluck. In his *Studies in Classic American Literature,* D. H. Lawrence, the coal miner's son, mocks Benjamin Franklin. Though Lawrence came from the working class, he remained an Englishman and it was necessary for him to forget the reason why Americans rebelled against the fatherland. Lawrence mocks Franklin's notion of a self-invented man—"The ideal man! And which is he, if you please?"—because Lawrence cannot enlarge upon the daunting, often comic task of self-invention. Free of the father, what is the American to do but imagine himself in the future tense? What could Ben grow up to become except an inventor? What figure could convey him but an aphorism?

Pity the rich man's son. The one thing most Americans think they know about the rich is that the rich are somehow deprived. Pity the rich man's son for never experiencing the keenness of privation. For never being his own man. So I believed when I was young and subscribed to the six crises of Richard Nixon. I knew that defeat was a greater test of character than victory. But there is another truth to America, much nearer to Tuscany. For all our professed admiration of the ascending narrative line, Americans often resent the awkwardness of arrival. When strife and fortitude end at a gaudy address or, worse, a bad lamp shade. Which is why self-made Americans from Pittsburgh and Cleveland in the nineteenth century needed to repair to Europe to learn boredom. Poor Richard, never so unattractive as when he gets to the top and finds everyone at the table silently regarding his demeanor. Look, they nudge one another: He's still hungry.

There was a book from some years ago called *Making It* by Norman Podhoretz. Yes, a notorious book. Podhoretz is not a man whose political pronouncements or whose political vendettas have sustained one's interest over the years. But on a bookstore shelf, even at the age I was—I was a man in my thirties—my hungry eyes must seize upon a title like *Making It*. My sort of book altogether, for being so candid about the boy's desire to advance. This was the story I loved to hear: The high school teacher who took young Podhoretz to a Fifth Avenue department store in order to purchase for our hero, with her own money, a black suit! Even more instructive than the book was its critical reception: "An embarrassment." The criticism came most fiercely from middle-aged men in New York, now at the top of their game, who had followed the same path; the first in their families to go to college (and the college was so often Harvard or CCNY). The consensus was that the book was unseemly.

When I published my first book, I wrote about my closet full of expensive suits. I characterized myself as moving with "the monstrous grace of the nouveau riche." This passage troubled my editor, the most thoroughgoing gentleman of my experience. "I don't think you want to say that," he wrote, "but it is up to you."

I wanted to say that, all right. I wanted to rid myself forever of the black suit. I would play Disraeli. I would play Edmund Kean. Brummell. But I would not arrive like some neurasthenic academic in a floorwalker's suit.

Whereas: Lyndon Johnson came from a past as humble as Nixon's, as humble as Franklin's, as humble as Lawrence's, as humble as my own. Johnson the populist, Johnson the signer of civil rights legislation, Johnson the militarist, Johnson would not have shared my embarrassment. Johnson was not handicapped by a sense of personal mission or divine election, or even lawful election. Though at first glance Johnson seems an American type, I believe he was less so than Nixon or Kennedy. I think Johnson would have been as intelligible within the loggia of the Medici or at Westminster or the Forbidden City. Wherever one goes, Johnson is already there. He was prepared to watch as the dangerous arrogance of the Kennedys played itself out.

Unlike Charles Dickens, D. H. Lawrence never imagined the happy accident of ascending to the upper classes. Lawrence sought spiritual transcendence among the Indians of New Mexico, away from the mechanical age.

I was a reader of the American novel. The foreground is where one came from. One puts on the black suit. In the distance lies the city—the Ivy League, the lukewarm cocktail; the good, worn carpet; the unwelcoming rich. I didn't want to know them, I wanted to be them—to have what they have. To know what they know. (Johnson only needed to know how much they knew.) Nixon believed in the same American novel. There he is in the foreground, dreaming of Kennedy in the distance. Perhaps even the Kennedys believed in the novel, or felt themselves exiled from the novel in which their father had taken such a rich advantage.

We know that Jack Kennedy and his sister would play the original cast album of *Finian's Rainbow* over and over through long afternoons—Ella Logan singing "How Are Things in Glocca Morra?" The not-quite-patricians harkening back to some distant dogpatch, yearning for the keenness of privation—a sentimental notion of the rich and the old. So perhaps young Kennedy read the novel backwards, which is history.

Johnson believed in the power of legislation to change history.

I think of Jack Kennedy, in the midst of family advisers—the brothers, the speechwriters, the lawyers, bluely, boozily, soberly scheming on the porch of a Cape Cod afternoon, deciding, I suppose, something like "the best direction for America." Such thought, such terms always seem to me more sinister than Nixon's solitary self-regard. The one thing rich Americans think they know about the poor is what the poor most urgently need (which never turns out to be money).

In the first televised presidential debate, Nixon thought he was upholding some puritan gravitas by refusing makeup; by choosing the citizen's black suit; choosing the poor man's version of natural aristocracy. Nixon was easily the more able in his grasp of history and the workings of government. John F. Kennedy, gold-dusted and ghostwritten, appeared completely natural. Nixon perspired.

In an instant, I saw what many other Americans saw that night: Harvard College will always beat Whittier College in America. The game is fixed and there is nothing to be done about it.

Then there were nights when the mood of the crowd changed at the wrestling matches. The barometer of the moment unaccountably plunged, as in a Dostoyevsky novel. Then the Okies and the Mexicans transferred allegiance away from the Joe Palooka hero—his golden curls and half-meloned chest. We were a fickle kind of Greek chorus. In that instant it was revealed to us that he was the liar, this so-called scientific wrestler, for he affected virtue in a game that was fixed. He was too elaborate in his inattention. He invented reasons to turn his back—feigned not to understand (his hand to his ear) the chorus's clear warning that the villain was sneaking up on him. (Ben Franklin: "Resolve to perform what you ought; perform without fail what you resolve.") *Boo!* The crowd began to appreciate the naturalness of the villain's response.

I am speaking of those years before the middle class took professional wrestling away from the working class and made of our morality play a mockery of ambition. I am speaking of those years when Gorgeous George intuited that spectators who knew so much disappointment might be inclined to laugh with the villain. Gorgeous George was immodest—hah, good for him!—he transformed the trappings of virtue to irony. His narcissism made it plain he was a bad'un. Thus he told the truth in a riddle of comic villainy.

For generations, Americans have been taught by teachers with straight faces and straitened incomes that anyone can do anything in America, can become anything they want to be.

After the grueling campaign of 1960, Nixon went down by the slimmest of margins. Had some deal been worked out between Old Man Kennedy and Mayor Daley? To his credit, Nixon accepted his fate and did not challenge the outcome. With his wife and two daughters, Nixon flew back to Washington. On the midnight of his return, Nixon built a fire in the library of his Washington house (thus realigning himself with the American myth of the midnight oil, with Franklin, with Lincoln), and counseled himself to think only of the future. "I knew that defeat was a greater test of character than victory."

Nixon's firelight reverie in *Six Crises* might be Franklin's, so plain is the regard of vicissitude: "In each of the crises of my political career, one lesson stood out: the period of greatest danger is not in preparing to meet a crisis or in fighting the battle itself but rather in that time immediately afterward, when the body, mind, and spirit are totally exhausted and there are still problems to deal with."

In 1962, Nixon was humbled enough by national defeat to lower his sights to California, where he ran for governor. At that time, I saw the man without his book. In Sacramento I watched a motorcade—NIXON FOR GOVERNOR—slowly advance along L Street. I stood close enough to the passing convertible to sustain Nixon's nervous glance for a moment, close enough to hear a curious patter that accompanied his dumb show recognition of the crowd; it was rhythmically akin to the catcher's taunt of *here batter batter.*

Later that year, Nixon played the villainous wrestler, losing sorely. He sneered at the gang of reporters assembled in the ballroom of the Beverly Hilton Hotel. Mrs. Nixon's face contorted to genuine grief, something Nixon could not manage. He could never portray himself, which is to say he could never conceal himself. His attempts at triumphal gesture were cruciform. His attempts to represent humility were triumphal. His uncontrolled facial muscles betrayed the passage of petty emotion—inappropriate simpers, pouts of chagrin. A sour-milk baby. Mr. Five O'Clock Shadow. I believe his pettiness showed that he cared, never more so than when he attempted to preempt the triumph of his critics: No Nixon to kick around anymore.

Nixon believed his own legend. He was the only one who did. Sentimentality is fatal for a politician, especially for a ruthless politician. Whereas I do not imagine Kennedy ever studied his own stride.

John Kennedy was slain in Dallas in 1963, a national tragedy that has since been downgraded to a back-street murder. His heroic body was laid to rest beneath an eternal flame. And the American novel, heretofore so comprehensible, momentarily took on unaccustomed themes. Was the novel to be about golden youth cut down? No, that wasn't a theme we recognized. Were there dark currents in America—factions that conspired against our light? We put on our black suits and we rehearsed our national pieties against such suspicions: America the novel—necessarily the child's story to write. Necessarily the truest sons and daughters of America are those born without, not the entitled sons with golden skins. You can be anything you want to be. Pity the rich man's son.

At the height of national mourning, Lyndon Johnson stepped forward, the man of no hour. Johnson was a natural man, no better than he should be. Johnson was a scientific wrestler—he marked his opponent's weaknesses and then waited for them. And Johnson rescued the American novel.

The Negro Civil Rights movement became, during Johnson's administration, the great American novel. Americans had to admit the game had been rigged for millions of its own citizens. What good were the plucky aphorisms of Poor Richard against the reality of racial exclusion? If America were to persist as a novel, then the opening chapter had to be repaired, at least to the extent that a black child could imagine Harvard in the distance. The revised opening chapter would henceforward be titled "Affirmative Action."

I remember that speech Johnson delivered at Howard University, in which he compared America to a footrace (a good Nixonian metaphor). "Freedom is not enough. . . . You do not take a person who, for years, has been hobbled by chains and liberate him, bring him up to the starting line of a race and then say, 'You are free to compete with all the others,' and still justly believe that you have been completely fair. . . . We seek not just freedom but opportunity . . . not just equality as a right and a theory but equality as a fact and equality as a result."

One Sunday afternoon in my sophomore year at Stanford, I was walking from the bus station to the campus. As I waited for the light to change, a student in a red Corvette asked if I wanted a lift. He wore dark glasses, he was blond, everything about him was blond. You cannot imagine anyone less confident than I was in college. But I did have some conversation. I could be quick-witted and curious. That afternoon, I silently watched with a raptor's eye the moving tendons of that golden arm. First gear. Second. Third. Radio dial. Jazz softly playing. I must have named my dorm. The only thing I remember saying was thank you as I climbed out. It wasn't anything. It was just the glamour of his easy generosity and his pity.

Privately, I redirected the object of education from learning how to be a scholarship boy to learning how not to be a scholarship boy. I wanted the grace of appearing not to want so much. What I did not know was how much *they* wanted. Like Nottingham. . . .

I knew who he was. Everyone knew who he was. Something to do with a fever. I read it in the school paper. He was dying. (Could I have read such a thing in the student newspaper?) He had been a champion swimmer—the young man with the improbable name. A fever he contracted where? But then, weeks after the febrile revelation, I saw him at the campus post office, calling for his mail. "Nottingham," he said to the clerk. He wasn't easily beautiful but one might train one's eye to prefer what he was. He was possessed of such grace.

What I didn't know about young men like Nottingham, men who had grown up in Woodside or Greenwich or Urbino, is that they had to train to become champion swimmers. There are probably thousands of young people in thousands of American high schools who do not realize this. We grow up thinking that the beautiful and the talented have been born that way, because they are born rich. The boys in the college gym with fine, muscular bodies—I thought they were athletes because of their bodies, not that their bodies were muscular because they were athletes. I thought I was the only one in the world who had to try so hard to become. Not someone like Nottingham. I saw in an instant he would not die.

The best advice I got at college was from a roommate who told me I should lose the black suit. He was an American who had grown up in Europe, so he was accustomed to studying what people wore. I certainly did not hear his advice as cruel. Black is for funerals, he said. You should try blue.

As well as taking up the Civil Rights movement, Lyndon Johnson took up Kennedy's war in Vietnam, a war he had no taste for; no imagination to know how to end. Johnson became a hated man in America.

In 1968, my parents bought our first color TV. Memory in America would henceforward be colored. Johnson turned gaunt, gray; changed from a vigorous opportunist to a man of sorrow. Richard Nixon—oddly, because everything about him was black; oddly, because he made a career of forbidding pink—Nixon was destined to be our first colorized president, elected because he promised to put an end to the lime and magenta war that burned day and night on TV screens. After Vietnam, telephones turned red, refrigerators green, ovens yellow.

Throughout the Johnson administration, domestic consideration of race remained black and white. Baptist hymns were converted to statistics. And since race, not social class, was the nation's most important metaphor for social division, Americans of every description were advancing their claims to government redress by analogy to Negro disadvantage.

Statistics were transposed back into hues and distributed along a black and white spectrum. In college, because of Lyndon Johnson, I became a "minority student." But it was not until Richard Nixon's administration that I became brown. A government document of dulling prose, Statistical Directive 15, would redefine America as an idea in five colors: White. Black. Yellow. Red. Brown.

To a generation of Americans—the first generation of affirmative action—these five categories became alternatives for any more subjective self-description. Cloaked in my official objective description—the black suit—I pursued the subjective.

Before Richard Nixon moved to the White House, I saw him, one very cold morning, departing his Fifth Avenue co-op (where the Rockefellers were also in residence); his head down, his mind on matters far from the shops and restaurants of Madison Avenue, his coat, his suit perfectly black, but I wish to put the emphasis on "perfectly" black, as black and as rich as a pelt. He looked a rich man that day. He seemed a lonely man. His body moved like a shadow, rather fantastically. Poor Richard, scrupulous Richard, pausing to look both ways before he crossed the one-way street, easily dismissed now as a petty criminal and thug, the dastardly black-caped villain of the penny melodrama, which he resembled—his finger to his lips as Americans hissed.

The dirty rassler.

In *Six Crises,* Nixon recalls that his mother, Hannah, prayed he might become a Quaker missionary to Central America. In a secular transposition of that vocation, Nixon ended up my godfather. Because of Nixon, several million Americans were baptized Hispanic.

After all that Richard Nixon had written about how hard work wins the day in America, finally it was Nixon who arranged for me to bypass the old rules. Through the agency of affirmative action, akin to those pivotal narrative devices in Victorian fictions, I had, suddenly, a powerful father in America, like Old Man Kennedy. I had, in short, found a way to cheat.

The saddest part of the story is that Nixon was willing to disown his own myth for political expediency. It would be the working-class white kid—the sort he had been—who would end up paying the price of affirmative action, not Kennedys. Affirmative action defined a "minority" in a numerical rather than a cultural sense. And since white males were already numerically "represented" in the boardroom, as at Harvard, the Appalachian white kid could not qualify as a minority. And since brown and black faces were "underrepresented," those least disadvantaged brown and black Americans, like me, were able to claim the prize of admission and no one questioned our progress.

Having betrayed his own memory of himself, it was at least dramatically appropriate that Nixon should betray his public annals. He taped himself for posterity; he taped every slander and bark.

You can overhear the unguarded Nixon, through earphones, through dense aural atmospheres, at "the Richard Nixon Birthplace and Library" in Yorba Linda, California. The tapes seem to me the least authentic version of Nixon extant. Is it my disappointment? From expressions Nixon used in public, like "all that love stuff" (describing rhetoric he shunned), one doesn't expect a fine conversation in the Nixon Oval Office. Still, from his books, I am convinced Nixon was not a coarse-grained man. Perhaps he was even delicate. Hannah Nixon used to joke that she had wanted a daughter. And she said about Nixon, her famous son, long after he had boarded the train and made something of himself in the world, "He was no child prodigy." But Hannah also remembered the way young Nixon needed her, as none of her other children did: "As a schoolboy, he used to like to have me sit with him when he studied. . . ."

Poor Richard. It is as though the Nixon on the tapes is talking the way he thinks "they" talk.

They don't.

They were appalled by him. When I was in graduate school, I spent a fall weekend in Sharon, Connecticut, with the wealthy parents of a school friend. These were people who knew several Nixon cabinet members socially, but disdained Nixon. One afternoon during that weekend, we drove to a cocktail party in a neighboring village. On our way, Chris's mother suggested we stop by to see Hotchkiss—"where Chris went to school." She had one of those Rosalind Russell accents. Such an accent should be trimmed with Indiana wit, and hers was. (She called her husband "Pa.") We turned through the gate. A vast lawn, strewn leaves, conformed to every novel of New England prep school life I had ever read. On cue, two golden boys dressed for lacrosse began to cross the green. I watched them with such concentration I feared my tongue might dart from my mouth.

Chris's mother in the front seat turned slightly: "Would you like to have come here?" she asked.

That is how they talk.

No.

No, I replied, and no I meant. No, I wouldn't be taunted so. (No, Ma.) Of course, I would like to have come here. Me and my black suit! And that is how *we* talk, Dickie. We say no too vehemently, admitting all.

The black suit? Oh, the spade, I think, rather than the club, rejoined the Duchess of Omnium, who had taken a pretty, well-proportioned drawing room in my novel-reading memory.

Josiah Franklin broke his son's heart because he could not purchase for his boy the finish of a good beginning. There were too many children in the family to afford Ben's education. I felt young Ben's disappointment as keenly as I'd felt Charles Dickens's horror of the blacking factory into which he'd been apprenticed by his family. Franklin's story, in my reading, confirmed the American faith in hard work. Not so Dickens's. The Dickensian hero was tossed by fate, must rely on a benefactor, some long-lost uncle, who steps from the crowd when our hero is most distressed and rescues him. In Dickens, fortune is the achievement of domestic bliss, a circumstance denied him personally. Dickens, like Nixon, became a national figure, and, of course, Dickens was beloved of the reading public of his time and since. But to the clubmen of his day, he remained a bit of a Cockney. Some called him that behind his back. The vest too elaborate, you see.

Myself as a child of fortune? Lyndon Johnson might do for the Victorian benefactor; was mine, in any case. During Johnson's administration I became eligible for affirming moneys. I did not initially question this diversion of my novel, and Richard Rodriguez, the child of fortune (by virtue of a cheap black suit), who thought his American entitlement came as a descendant of Benjamin Franklin—"our forefathers," he had been taught to say, and he believed it!—Richard progressed in a direction more British than American.

Ben Franklin would never have qualified for affirmative action; would never have, thus, been ransomed from the candle shop. Possibly, as a poor white skinhead, Franklin would have joined a seditious citizens' militia or become an Internet pamphleteer. None of them would have qualified—Franklin, Johnson, Nixon.

My election saw me through the last years of graduate school—and beyond, to this very page.

Where I am invited to speak at high schools and colleges. I hear myself dispensing Franklinian advice. *Make yourself a goal. Don't let the neighborhood define you. Find out what lies on the other side of town. Read! Change!* My Franklinian optimism cloaks years of Nixonian observation.

The most important thing I learned in college about the rich is that they pursue hobbies.

The best advice I ever got about America didn't come from Richard Nixon or Benjamin Franklin or from any college lecture or book. It came from a Southern California divorcée who had fallen off her high heels. "Never, never ask the rich for anything. If you are invited onto the private jet, okay. Just don't ask for cab fare to the airport."

The Nixon library at Yorba Linda, California, is sentimental, amoral, collects everything, but assigns no value. The ephemeral, the vulgar, the embarrassing, even the criminal: a couple of surprisingly good paintings, the presidential limousine, the inaugural Bible; the Refusal to Be Deposed. I suppose you would say it is tasteless. A bad architecture. Employees dressed in red, white, and blue. Box lunches. A First Lady's Rose Garden.

Even so, I find in middle age I prefer the plain precepts of Whittier College to the noblesse oblige of Harvard. I hate it when Harvard wins. The winners win.

A young man who works in the gift shop has a pierced ear. The ring has been removed. There is one example of conscious camp that results in a potent nostalgia: All documentary films are shown on vintage television sets. The single concession to postmodern California is some landscaper's impulse to plant borders of lavender. But someone else has come along to Republicanize the lavender impulse; has sidewalled it and topped it like privet. The guards are spooky, their walkie-talkie vigilance suggests only crackpots visit this tomb.

The only other tourists this day are Taiwanese. They came in a bus. They are interested in the house—"the Birthplace" (something oddly Maoist in the signage). The Birthplace enshrines "the piano." Nixon played the piano slavishly because music is good for one. Hard to believe arch-criminality ascribed to a man whose imagination was so perfunctorily furnished. Here are the three instruments he "mastered"—according to the docent—clarinet, violin, piano.

The boy who dreamed his escape on a train whistle floating east, ended up in a gated New Jersey suburb redrawing the map of the world. The world was his last invention. Odd that this self-made man who spent so much time with his long nose to the grindstone would evolve into the global seer, scholar of the world, statesman, not least a politician who wrote his own books.

In a late interview, Frank Gannon asked Nixon if he believed he had lived a "good life." Nixon replied, "I don't get into that kind of crap." But what did he truly think in the end? His fall was as precipitous as any in American history. Did he suppose he had fallen too low to recover? Or did he allow himself to imagine a day when his fortunes might yet be reversed? With perseverance. With pluck. With a library.

The Resting Place is not far from the Birthplace, across a small pathway. No eternal flame here. *None of that love stuff.* Two flat markers. Grass. Richard Nixon. Patricia Nixon. Some precept or quote upon each. Hers is something inane, desperate, trustworthy, from a speech she once gave in a dark country. "Even when people can't speak your language, they can tell if you have love in your heart."

His reads like a fortune cookie. "The greatest honor history can bestow is the title of peacemaker."

One can imagine a version of Richard Nixon here in Yorba Linda. Young. Awkward. Self-effacing. Embarrassed. Friendly. But one cannot imagine the man who became great and dark-minded. For it was in his mind the suit lodged.

The end of the day. Philadelphia in the young nation. Lamps lit and the sound of an old horse pulling a cart over cobblestones. *Evening. Put things in their places. Supper. Music or diversion, or conversation. Examination of the day.*

Sleep.

■ *Chapter Five* ■

HISPANIC

Hi.spa´.nick. 1. Spanish, *adjective.* 2. Latin American, *adjective.* 3. Hispano, *noun.* An American citizen or resident of Spanish descent. 4. Ducking under the cyclone fence, *noun.* 5. Seen running from the scene of the crime, *adjective.* Clinging to a raft off the Florida coast. Elected mayor in New Jersey. Elevated to bishop or traded to the San Diego Padres. Awarded the golden pomegranate by the U.S. Census Bureau: "most fertile." Soon, an oxymoron: America's largest minority. An utter absurdity: "destined to outnumber blacks." A synonym for the future (salsa having replaced catsup on most American kitchen tables). Madonna's daughter. Sammy Sosa's son. Little Elián and his Great Big Family. A jillarioso novel about ten sisters, their sorrows and joys and intrauterine devices. The new face of American Protestantism: Evangelical minister, tats on his arms; wouldn't buy a used car from. Highest high school dropout rate; magical realism.

The question remains: Do Hispanics exist?

I tell myself, on mornings like this—the fog has burned off early—that I am really going to give it up. Hispanicism cannot interest me anymore. My desk a jumble of newspaper clippings. Look at all this! Folders. It looks like a set for *The Makropolous Case*. I will turn instead to the death agony of a moth, the gigantic shuddering of lantern-paper wings. Or I will count the wrinkles on Walden Pond. I will write some of those constipated, low-paying, fin de siècle essays about the difficulty of *saying* anything in this, our age. *Visi d'arte*, from now on, as Susan Sontag sang so memorably from the chapel of Sant'Andrea della Valle.

For years now I have pursued Hispanicism, as a solitary, self-appointed inspector in an old Hitchcock will dog some great hoax; amassing data; abstractedly setting down his coffee cup at a precarious angle to its saucer, to the stack of papers and books and maps on which it rests, because he is drawn to some flash-lit, spyglassed item in the morning paper. I am catching them up, slowly, inexorably, confident of the day—soon—when I shall publish my findings.

Soon. I take my collapsible double-irony on tour to hotel ballroom conferences and C-SPAN-televised luncheons and "Diversity Week" lectures at universities. For a fee, I rise to say I am not Latin American, because I am Hispanic. I am Hispanic because I live in the United States. *Thank you.* (For a larger fee, I will add there is no such thing as a Hispanic. *Thank you.*)

But this morning I have decided, after all, to join the hoax.

Hispanic has had its way with me. I suspect also with you. The years have convinced me that Hispanic is a noun that can't lose. An adjective with legs. There is money in it.

Hispanic (the noun, the adjective) has encouraged the Americanization of millions of Hispanics. But at the same time, Hispanic—the ascending tally announced by the U.S. Census Bureau—has encouraged the Latinization of non-Hispanics.

As a Hispanic, as a middle-aged noun, like Oscar Wilde descending to gaol, I now take my place in the booth provided within that unglamorous American fair devised by the Richard Nixon administration in 1973 (O.M.B. Statistical Directive 15). Within the Nixonian fair are five exposition halls:

BLACK;
WHITE;
ASIAN/PACIFIC ISLANDER;
NATIVE AMERICAN/ESKIMO;
HISPANIC.

They aren't much, these drafty rooms—about what you'd expect of government issue. Nixon's fair attempted to describe the world that exists by portraying a world that doesn't. Statisticians in overalls moved India—*ouffff*—that heavy, spooled and whirligigged piece of Victorian mahogany, over beneath the green silk tent of Asia. Mayan Indians from the Yucatán were directed to the Hispanic pavilion (Spanish colonial), which they must share with Argentine tangoistas, Colombian drug dealers, and Russian Jews who remember Cuba from the viewpoint of Miami. Of the five ports, Hispanic has the least reference to blood. There is no such thing as Hispanic blood. (*Do I not bleed?*) Though I meet young Hispanics who imagine they descend from it.

Nixon's fair does at least succeed in portraying the United States in relation to the world. One can infer a globe from a pentagram.

Over my head, as I write these words, a New World Indian is singing in the language of the conquistador. (A Korean contractor, hired by my landlord, has enlisted a tribe of blue-jumpered Mexican Indians to reroof the apartment building where I live.) In trustworthy falsetto, the young man lodges a complaint against an intangible mistress unfond, as high above him as the stars, and as cold. Yesterday, as he was about to hoist a roll of tar paper, this same young man told me the choir of roofers, excepting *"el patron,"* originate from a single village in a far state of Mexico. And a few minutes ago, I overheard them all—the Mexicans and the Korean contractor—negotiating their business in pidgin (Spanish, curiously; I would have expected English). Then my ceiling shook with their footfalls. And with bolts of tar paper flung upon it. My library leapt in its shelves— those ladies and gentlemen, so unaccustomed.

Tomorrow, having secured my abstractions against the rainy season, the Mexican Indians will fly away to some other rooftop in the city, while I must remain at this desk.

Why must I? Because my literary agent has encouraged from me a book that answers a simple question: *What do Hispanics mean to the life of America?* He asked me that question several years ago in a French restaurant on East Fifty-seventh

Street, as I watched a waiter approach our table holding before
him a shimmering *îles flottantes*.

▪ ▪ ▪

But those were palmier days. Before there were Hispanics in
America, there was another fictitious, inclusive genus: the Latin
Lover. The Latin Lover was male counterpart to the vamp. He
specialized in the inarticulate—"dark"—passions; perhaps a
little cruel. He was mascaraed, mute, prepotent. Phantom,
sheikh, or matador, he was of no philosophy but appetite. His
appetite was blond.

White America's wettest perdition fantasy has always been
consanguinity with some plum-colored thigh. The Latin Lover
was a way of meeting the fantasy halfway. This was not a complicated scenario. Nor was Hollywood fussy about casting it.
Ramon Navarro, Rudolph Valentino, Ezio Pinza, Rossano
Brazzi, Ricardo Montalban, Prince Rainier, George Chakiris,
all descended from the dusky isles of Cha-Cha.

Probably the last unironic Latin Lover conscripted into American fantasy was Omar Sharif, hired to seduce Peter O'Toole.

But, by then, Lucille Ball had undermined the fantasy by do-
mesticating the Latin Lover. In the 1950s, Lucille Ball insisted
upon casting her real-life husband as her fictional husband,
against the advice of CBS Television executives. Desi Arnaz
was not mute, nor were his looks smoldering. In fact his eyes
bulged with incredulity at *la vida loca* with Lucy. Curiously,
Lucy was the madcap for having married a Cuban bandleader
in the first place. Curiously, Desi was the solid American citi-

zen (though he did wear a smoking jacket at home). Soon, millions of Americans began a Monday night vigil, awaiting the birth of Little Ricky, the first Hispanic.

By the time *I Love Lucy* went to divorce court, Desi Arnaz had been replaced on our television screens by Fidel Castro. Castro was a perverted hotblood—he was a cold warrior—as was his Byronic sidekick, Ché. Our fantasy toyed for a time with what lay beneath the beards. When we eventually got a translation, we took fright. *Bad wolf!* Rhetoric too red for our fantasy.

The red wolf ripped away the Copacabana curtain—all the nightclub gaity of Latin America in old black-and-white movies—to reveal a land of desperate want.

In the early 1960s, Mexican Americans were described by American liberals as an "invisible minority." Americans nevertheless saw farmworkers in the Central Valley of California singing and praying in Spanish. Americans later saw angry Chicanos on TV imitating the style of black militancy.

By the 1970s, even as millions of Latin Americans came north, seeking their future as capitalists, the Latin Lover faded from America's imagination.

▪ ▪ ▪

Surviving Chicanos (one still meets them) scorn the term Hispanic, in part because it was Richard Nixon who drafted the noun and who made the adjective uniform. Chicanos resist the term, as well, because it reduces the many and complicated stories of the Mexican in America to a mere chapter of a much larger saga that now includes Hondurans and Peruvians and Cubans. Chicanos resent having to share mythic space with parvenus and numerically lesser immigrant Latin American populations. After all, Mexican Americans number more than seventy percent of the nation's total Hispanics. And, Chicanos say, borrowing a tabula rasa from American Indians, we are not just another "immigrant" population in the United States. We were here before the *Mayflower*. Which is true enough, though "we" and "here" are blurred by imprecision. California was once Mexico, as were other parts of the Southwestern United States. So we were here when here was there. In truth, however, the majority of Mexican Americans, or our ancestors, crossed a border.

One meets Hispanics who refuse Hispanic because of its colonial tooling. Hispanic, they say, places Latin America (once more) under the rubric of Spain. An alternate noun the disaffected prefer is "Latino," because they imagine the term locates them in the Americas, which the term now does in all revised American dictionaries, because Latinos insist that it does. (What is language other than an agreement, like Greenwich Mean Time?) In fact, Latino commits Latin America to Iberian memory as surely as does Hispanic. And Latino is a Spanish word, thus also paying linguistic obeisance to Spain. For what, after all, does "Latin" refer to, if not the imperial root system?

Hispanicus sui.

My private argument with Latino is no more complicated than my dislike for a dictation of terms. I am Latino against my will: I write for several newspapers—the *Los Angeles Times* most often—papers that have chosen to warrant "Latino" over "Hispanic" as correct usage. The newspaper's computer becomes sensitive, not to say jumpy, as regards correct political usage. Every Hispanic the computer busts is digitally repatriated to Latino. As I therefore also become.

In fact, I do have a preference for Hispanic over Latino. To call oneself Hispanic is to admit a relationship to Latin America in English. *Soy* Hispanic is a brown assertion.

Hispanic nativists who, of course, would never call themselves Hispanic, nonetheless have a telling name for their next-door neighbors who are not Hispanic. The word is "Anglo." Do Irish Americans become Anglos? And do you suppose a Chinese American or an African American is an Anglo? Does the term define a group of Americans by virtue of a linguistic tie to England or by the lack of a tie to Spain? (Come now, think. Did no one in your family take a Spanish course? In high school?) In which case, the more interesting question becomes whether Hispanics who call Anglos Anglo are themselves Anglo?

Nevertheless, in a Texas high school, according to the *Dallas Morning News*, a gang of "Anglos" and a gang of "Hispanics" shed real blood in a nonfictional cafeteria, in imitation of a sixteenth-century sea battle the students doubtlessly never heard of. Who could have guessed that a European rivalry would play itself out several hundred years after Philip's Armada was sunk by Elizabeth's navie? And here? No other country in the world has been so confident of its freedom from memory. Yet Americans comically (because unknowingly) assume proxy roles within a centuries-old quarrel of tongues.

▪ ▪ ▪

Englande and España divided much of the Americas between them. England gave her colonial territories a remarkable code of civil law, a spectacular literature, a taste for sweeties, and the protean pronoun that ushered in the modern age—"I"—the lodestar for Protestant and capitalist and Hispanic memoirist. Counter-Reformation Spain gave its New World possessions *nosotros*—the cupolic "we"—an assurance of orthodoxy, baroque, fugue, smoke, sunglasses, and a piquant lexicon for miscegenation. Every combination of races is accounted for in New World Spanish. (Except Hispanic.) (Or Latino.)

The numerical rise of the Hispanic in the United States occasioned language skirmishes, especially in those parts of the country where the shadow of Philip's crown once crossed Elizabeth's scepter. On the one hand, in the 1960s, Chicano neo-nationalists attempted to make "bilingual education" the cornerstone of their political agenda, since little other than tongue (and not even that oftentimes) united Hispanics. Anglo nativists distributed ballots to establish English as "the official language of the United States." In truth, America is a more complicated country than either faction dares admit.

Americans do not speak "English." Even before our rebellion against England, our tongue tasted of Indian—*succotash, succotash,* we love to say it; *Mississippi,* we love to spell. We speak American. Our tongue is not something slow and mucous that plods like an oyster through its bed in the sea, afearing of taint or blister. Our tongue sticks out; it is a dog's tongue, an organ of curiosity and science.

The history of a people—their hungers, weathers, kinships,

humors, erotic salts and pastimes—gets told by turns of phrase. Which is why the best history of the United States I ever read is not a history of battles and presidents and such, but H. L. Mencken's *The American Language*, an epic of nouns and verbs and proverbs; things we pick up or put down by name.

By 1850, William C. Fowler was describing "American dialects." Nine years later, John Russell Bartlett offered a glossary of "words and phrases usually regarded as peculiar to the United States": archaisms, et cetera. The American tongue created what Russell called "negroisms"—cadences, inflections, parodies, refusals. Our lewd tongue partook of everything that washed over it; everything that it washed—even a disreputable history. That is how young Walt Whitman heard America singing in the nineteenth century, heard the varied carols of trade in old New York harbor, heard young fellows, robust, friendly, singing with open mouths.

Nativists who want to declare English the official language of the United States do not understand the omnivorous appetite of the language they wish to protect. Neither do they understand that their protection would harm our tongue. (A restaurant in my neighborhood advertises "Harm on Rye.") Those Americans who would build a fence around American English to forestall the Trojan burrito would turn American into a frightened tongue, a shrinking little oyster tongue, as French has lately become, priested over by the Ancients of the Académie, who fret so about *le weekend*.

In an essay published in *Harper's* of April 1917, an immigrant son, M. E. Ravage, complained about the way Americans lick the oak leaves and acorns off the old monikers, so that they became "emasculated and devoid of either character or meaning. Mordecai—a name full of romantic association—had been changed to the insipid monosyllable Max. Rebecca—mother of the race—was in America Becky. Samuel had been shorn to Sam, Abraham to Abe, Israel to Izzy."

How Ricardo became rich: When I was new to this tongue I now include myself in, I learned some things that were true about America from its corn, its speed, its disinclination to be tied down, pretty much; its inclination toward shortcuts, abbreviations, sunwise turns. I learned from "hi" and "nope" and "OK." We Americans like the old, rubbed phrases; we like better the newest, sassiest, most abbreviated: Y2K. The most bubulous American word I learned early on was the unexpected word for one's father (though not mine) and soda and what the weasel goes: pop.

I observed parents laughing over their children's coinages. I inferred the burden and responsibility of each adolescent generation to come up with neat subversions; to reinvent adolescence in a patois inscrutable to adults. The older generation expected it.

But not in my family. My mother and father (with immigrant pragmatism) assumed the American tongue would reinvent their children. Just so did several immigrant Hispanic mothers in Southern California recently remark their children's reluctance to join America. These mothers feared their children were not swimming in the American current—not in the swifts and not in the depths; not even in the pop. They blamed "bilingual education," a leaky boat theorem ostensibly designed to sink into the American current. (In fact, the theorem became a bureacracy preoccupied with prolonging itself.) These few mothers organized an opposition to bilingual education and eventually they sank the Armada in California. Theirs was an American impulse: to engage the American flow directly and to let their children be taken by it.

But the American current always fears itself going dry—it longs, always, for a wetter wah-wah (there used to be a night club called "King Tut's Wah-Wah Hut"); yearns now to swizzle Latin America in its maw. Spanish is becoming unofficially but truly the second language of the United States. Moreover, Yankee pragmatism accomplishes the romance of the American tongue. By the 1980s, advertising executives in L.A. and Miami were the first to describe the United States as "the fifth-largest Spanish-speaking market in the world." Pragmatism made Spanish the language of cheap labor from fishing villages in Alaska to Chinese restaurants in Georgia to my rooftop here in San Francisco.

Thus does official America now communicate in at least two "voices," like a Tuva singer; three in Eurasian San Francisco. And if it isn't entirely English, it is nevertheless entirely American.

Press ONE, if you wish to continue in English. Pragmatism leads to Spanish signage at government offices, hospitals, parking lots, bus stops, polls. Telephone instructions, prescription instructions, microwave instructions—virtually all instructions in America are in Spanish as well as English.

American politicians, too, begin to brush up their Yanqui-Dudel.

I remain skeptical of the effect pragmatic Spanish might have on the assimilation of Latin American immigrants. Working-class newcomers from Latin America do not suffer the discontinuity that previous generations used to propel themselves into the future tense. But middle-class Americans, friends of mine, composites of friends of mine, of a liberal bent, nice people, OK people, see nothing wrong with bilingual education. In fact, they wish their own children to be bilingual. In fact, they send their kids to French schools. In fact, they ask if I know of a housekeeper who might inadvertently teach their children Spanish while she dusts under the piano.

Nope.

But I marvel at the middle-class American willingness to take Spanish up. Standing in the burrito line in a Chinese neighborhood, I notice how many customers know the chopsticks of Spanish: "carnitas" and "guacamole" and "sí," "gracias," "refritos," and "caliente," and all the rest of what they need to know. And it occurs to me that the Chinese-American couple in front of me, by speaking Spanish, may actually be speaking American English.

On an American Airlines flight to New York, I listen to the recorded bilingual safety instructions. "She" speaks in cheerful, speedo, gum-scented American English. "He" partners her every unlikely event in Spanish; makes tragedy sound a tad less unlikely. (The Latin Lover speaks, I think to myself.)

Some years ago, I stood on a bluff on the San Diego side of

the U.S.–Mexico border, watching Latin American peasants bent double and yet moving rapidly through the dark. I experienced something like the confounding stasis one dislikes in those Escher prints where the white birds fly east as the black birds fly west and the gray birds seem unformed daubs of marzipan. Was I watching the past become the future or the future becoming the past?

Back in the 1960s, Chicano activists referred to the "reconquista" of the United States, by which they meant the Southwest was becoming, again, Spanish-speaking, as it had been in the 1840s (history, therefore, a circle, and not, as America had always insisted, a straight line). Then again I might be watching an advance of the Spanish crown—Latin American peasants as cannon fodder for the advance of King Philip II; spies in cloaks who will insinuate themselves into Anglo households to whisper Ave Marias into baby's shell-like ear.

Sitting on American Airlines flight 64, I am not so sure. The numbers of Latin American immigrants making their way into the United States more truly honor England. Millions of Latin Americans, my parents among them, have come to the United States because of the enduring failures of Father Spain. Their coming honors England.

Her face painted white, she receives the passenger list into her gem-encrusted hand, but does not look upon it.

The Armada sank, ma'am.

There is glint in her simian eye. Lips recede from tallow teeth to speak:

They are trumped, then, My Lord Admiral.

The airplane shudders down the runway, hoisting sail.

▪ ▪ ▪

What did Nixon know? Did he really devise to rid himself of a bunch of spic agitators by officially designating them a minority, entitled to all rights, honors, privileges, and obligations thereto appertaining: rhetorical flatteries, dollars, exploding cigars? (Maybe, by the same token, he could put blacks on notice that they were no longer such a hot ticket.)

A young Bolivian in Portland giggled, oh quite stupidly, at my question, her hand patting her clavicle as if she held a fan. I had asked her whether she had yet become Hispanic. Perhaps she didn't understand the question.

In *The Next American Nation*, Michael Lind observes that "real Hispanics think of themselves not as generic Hispanics, but as Mexicans, or Puerto Ricans or Cubans or Chileans." Lind is wrong. Well, he is right in the past tense; he is wrong in the future. You won't find Hispanics in Latin America (his point)—not in the quickening cities, not in the emasculated villages. You need to come to the United States to meet Hispanics (my point). What Hispanic immigrants learn within the United States is to view themselves in a new way, as belonging to Latin America entire—precisely at the moment they no longer do.

America's brilliance is a lack of subtlety. Most Americans are soft on geography. We like puzzles with great big pieces, pie-crust coasts. And we're not too fussy about the midlands. But American obliviousness of the specific becomes a gift of prophesy regarding the approaching mass. Our impatience has created the map of the future. Many decades before Germans spoke of the EEC or the French could imagine buying french fries with Euros, Americans spoke of "Europe" (a cloud bank, the Eiffel Tower, the Colosseum, any decorative ormolu, inventing the place in novels and government reports, blurring borders and tongues and currencies and Prussians and Talleyrands into an abstraction, the largest unit, the largest parenthesis that can yet contain onion domes, Gothic spires, windmills, gondolas, bidets, and the *Mona Lisa*).

Many European men, such as the gondolier in Venice, come home from work to eat their noonday meals (according to an American social studies textbook, c. 1959).

Similarly, and for many generations, slaves and the descendants of slaves in America invented a homeland called "Africa"—a land before slave ships, a prelapsarian savanna whereupon the provocatively dressed gazelle could stroll safely after dark. Perhaps someday Africa will exist, in which case it will have been patented by African Americans in the U.S.A. from the example of the American Civil Rights movement. Yes, and lately I have begun to meet people in the United States who call themselves "Asians." A young woman (a Vietnamese immigrant) tells me, for instance, she will only "date Asian." Asians do not exist anywhere in Asia. The lovely brown woman who has cared for my parents, a Mormon born on an island in a turtle-green sea (I've guessed the Philippines or Samoa), will only admit to "Pacific Islander." A true daughter of Nixon.

It is not mere carelessness that makes Americans so careless, it is also that Americans think more about the future than the past. The past is vague to us. Tribal feuds may yet hissle and spit on the stoves of somebody's memory, but we haven't

got time for that. The entry guard at Ellis Island didn't have
time for that. The INS official at LAX doesn't have time for
that. He is guarding the portal to individualism, the greatest
abstraction the world has ever known: *One at a time, one at
a time—back up, sir!* Only America could create Hispanics,
Asians, Africans, Americans.

*The Chinese people are like Americans in many ways.
They like to laugh and be happy and play games.* (Same
American social studies textbook, c. 1959.)

It was only when it came to the landmass extending from
Tierra del Fuego to the Aleutians that Americans refused to
think in terms of hemispheric or historical mass. America (the
noun) became our border against all that lay to the south and
north—much to the annoyance of Mexicans, for example, or
Canadians. "We are Americans, too," they said. No you're not,
you are Mexicans. And you are Canadians. We are Ameri-
cans©.

Whereas Miss Bolivia, having gotten over herspanic and
now surreptitiously refreshing her lip gloss, does, as it turns
out, understand my question. She is not Hispanic. Ha ha no.
What is she then?

Her eyes flash. I mean, what do you consider yourself to be?
¡Bolivian!

Of course, but I protest she is destined for Hispanicity. Because you live in the United States, you see.

¿?

You will know more Colombians and Nicaraguans as friends,
fellow religionists, than you would have known had you never

left Bolivia. Spanish-language radio and TV, beamed at immigrants of provincial memory, will parlay soccer scores from an entire hemisphere. You will hear weather reports from Valparaiso to Anchorage borne on a dolphin-headed breeze. Listen, chaste Miss Bolivia: All along the dial, north and south, on Spanish-language radio stations, you can already hear a new, North American Spanish accent—akin to "accentless" California TV English—meant to be decipherable (and inoffensive) alike to Cubans, Mexicans, Dominicans, and blonds like you, because it belongs to none.

Hispanic Spanish is hybrid, uniform. Colorless, yes. I do not deplore it. If I were Miss Bolivia, I might deplore it. One should deplore any loss of uniquity in a world that has so little. But I take the bland transparent accent as an anabranch of the American tongue. We bid fond farewell to Miss Bolivia. Who's our next contestant, Johnny?

The Cuban grandfather in Miami, Dick, who persists in mocking Mexicans because we are Indians, less European than he is, the old frog. We've put him in a soundproof booth so his Hispanic grandson can mimic for us the old man's Caribbean Spanish, filigreed as a viceroy's sleeve.

▪ ▪ ▪

I think Richard Nixon would not be surprised to hear that some of my Hispanic nieces and nephews have Scottish or German surnames. Nixon intended his Spanish'd noun to fold Hispanics into America. By the time the Sunday supplements would begin writing about the political ascendancy of a Hispanic generation, the American children of that generation would be disappearing into America. But Nixon might be surprised to hear that my oldest nephew, German-surnamed, has a restaurant in Oakland dedicated to classic Mexican cooking; the majority of his customers are not Hispanic.

In generations past, Americans regarded Latin America as an "experiment in democracy," meaning the brutish innocence of them, the negligent benevolence of us, as defined by the Monroe Doctrine. We installed men with dark glasses to overthrow men with dark glasses.

As a result of Nixon's noun, our relationship to Latin America became less remote. Within our own sovereign borders, crested with eagles, twenty-five million became twenty-seven million Hispanics; became thirty-five million. The Census Bureau began making national predictions: By the year 2040 one in three Americans will declare herself Hispanic. Leaving aside the carbonated empiricism of such predictions, they nevertheless did convince many Americans that Latin America is no longer something "down there," like an adolescent sexual abstraction. By the reckoning of the U.S. Census Bureau, the United States has become one of the largest Latin American nations in the world.

And every day and every night poor people trample the legal fiction that America controls its own destiny. There is something of inevitability, too, in what I begin hearing in America from businessmen—a hint of Latin American fatalism, a recognition of tragedy that is simply the verso of optimism, but descriptive of the same event: *You can't stop them coming* becomes *the necessity to develop a Spanish-language ad strategy.*

The mayor of San Diego, speaking to me one morning several years ago about her city's relationship to Tijuana, about the proximity of Tijuana to San Diego, used no future tense—*Here we are,* she said. She used no hand gesture to indicate "they" or "there" or "here." The mayor's omission of a demonstrative gesture in that instance reminded me of my father's nonchalance. My father never expected to escape tragedy by escaping Mexico, by escaping poverty, by coming to the United States. Nor did he. Such sentiments—the mayor's, my father's—are not, I remind you, the traditional sentiments of an "I" culture, which would formulate the same proximity as *"right up to here."* For my father, as for the mayor, the border was missing.

In old cowboy movies, the sheriff rode hell-for-leather to capture the desperados before they crossed the Rio Grande. It is an old idea, more Protestant than Anglo-Saxon: that Latin America harbors outlaws.

Some Americans prefer to blame the white-powder trail leading from here to there on the drug lords of Latin America. More Americans are beginning to attribute the rise of drug traffic to American addiction. Tentative proposals to legalize drugs, like tentative proposals to open the border, bow to the inevitable, which is, in either case, the knowledge that there is no border.

The other day I read a survey that reported a majority of Americans believe most Hispanics are in the United States illegally. Maybe. Maybe there is something inherently illegal about all of us who are Hispanics in the United States, gathered under an assumed name, posing as one family. Nixon's categorical confusion brings confusion to all categories.

Once the United States related millions of its citizens into the family Hispanic—which as a legality exists only within U.S. borders—then that relation extends back to our several origins and links them. At which juncture the U.S.A. becomes the place of origin for all Hispanics. The illegal idea now disseminated southward by the U.S. is the idea that all Latin Americans are Hispanic.

The United States has illegally crossed its own border.

Chapter Six

THE THIRD MAN

A CHINESE OR AN ESKIMO OR A COUNTERTENOR COULD PLAY this role as well. Anyone in America who does not describe himself as black or white can take the role. But the reason I am here, on this dais, in a hotel ballroom, is numerical.

Our subject today is the perennial American subject: Race Relations. You understand, by this time, I am not a race. I do not have a race. To my left, standing at the microphone, is an African-American academic who refers to himself as "black." To my right sits a journalist who calls himself "white." My role is the man in the middle, the third man; neither.

Situated thus, between black and white—occupying the passing lane in American demographics—the Hispanic should logically be gray or at least a blur.

Americans dislike gray. Gray areas, gray skies, gray flannel suits, mice, hair, cities, seas. Moscow. Hera's eyes.

But I am not gray, I am brown as you can see, or rather you can't see, but my name on this book is brown. Rodriguez is a brown name—or gray—halfway between Greenwich and Timbuktu. I am brown all right—darkish reddish, terra-cotta-ish, dirt-like, burnt Sienna in the manner of the middle Bellini.

At the microphone, the African-American professor refers (in one breath) to "blacks-and-Latinos," his synonym for the disadvantaged in America—the dropout, the lost, the under-arrest. The professor's rhetorical generosity leaves me abashed.

In truth, African Americans are in fierce competition with Hispanics in this country. We compete for the meanest jobs or for the security of civil service positions or for political office or for white noise. If I were an African American I would not be so generous toward Hispanics, especially if I had to read every morning of their ascending totals. The *Wall Street Journal*, March 8, 2001: NUMBER OF HISPANICS BALLOONED IN 1990S; GROUP IS ABOUT TO BECOME BIGGEST MINORITY. I would resent the incurious gabble of Spanish invading African-American neighborhoods; Hispanics demanding from the federal government the largest slice of black metaphor; and this—my brown intrusion into the tragic dialectic of America, the black and white conversation.

Not so long ago, Hispanics, particularly Mexicans and Cubans, resisted the label of "minority." In a black-and-white America, Hispanics tended toward white, or at least tended to keep their distance from black. I remember my young Mexican mother saying to her children, in Spanish, "We are not minorities," in the same voice she would use decades later to refuse the term "senior citizen." One day in the 1980s, my mother became a senior citizen because it got her on the bus for a nickel. One day, in the 1960s, the success of the Negro Civil Rights movement encouraged Hispanics (along with other groups of Americans) to insist on the coveted black analogy, and thus claim the spoils of affirmative action.

Today you will see us listed on surveys and charts, between Black and White, as though Hispanics are necessarily distinct from either Black or White; as though Hispanics are comparable to either Black or White.

Out of mischief or stupidity, federal demographers have taken to predicting that Hispanics are destined to replace African Americans as "American's largest minority." The Census Bureau manages both to trivialize the significance of Hispanics to our national life, and to insult African Americans by describing Hispanics as supplanters. To date, the nation's Hispanic political leadership has remained silent about the Census Bureau's grammar.

The notion of African Americans as a minority is one born of a distinct and terrible history of exclusion—the sin of slavery, later decades of segregation, and every conceivable humiliation visited upon a people, lasting through generations. To say, today, that Hispanics are becoming America's largest minority is to mock history, to pervert language, to dilute the noun "minority" until it means little more than a population segment.

This is exactly what Hispanics have become—a population segment, an ad-agency target audience, a market share. Not coincidentally, it was an advertising agency that got the point of

Hispanic totals as early as the 1980s. It was then that Coors Beer erected billboards throughout the Southwest that flattered "The Decade of the Hispanic."

By telling you these things, I do not betray "my people." I think of the nation entire—all Americans—as my people. Though I call myself Hispanic, I see myself within the history of African Americans and Irish Catholics and American Jews and the Chinese of California.

When citizens feel themselves excluded, it is appropriate that they lobby, petition, attract the interest of government and employers. But when Americans organize into subgroups, it should be with an eye to merging with the whole, not remaining separate. What was the point of the Negro Civil Rights movement of the early twentieth century, if not integration?

The trouble with today's ethnic and racial and sexual identifications is that they become evasions of citizenship. Groups beget subgroups: Last week in Atlanta there was a meeting of Colombian Americans, their first convention. In parody of Hispanics nationally, Colombian Americans declared themselves to be "America's fastest-growing minority."

At Yale University, I was recently trailed by a white graduate student—truly Hispanic—who kept boasting that she was the "first Latina to win" and the "first Latina named." The moment we sat down to talk, this white Hispanic referred to herself as "a person of color" and I realized she had no idea.

Alone among the five (White, Black, Asian, et cetera) options placed at one's disposal on affirmative action applications, Hispanic is the only category that has no reference to blood. One can be an Asian Hispanic or an Indian Hispanic, et cetera. Indeed, I know Hispanics who are of a complexion most Americans would call black but who elect to name themselves Hispanic. I know Hispanics who are blithe as daffodils.

Here is what I will say when it is my turn to get up and speak: *Hispanicity is culture. Not blood. Not race. Culture, or the illusion of culture—ghost-ridden. A belief that the dead have a hold on the living.*

What I will not say, when I get up to speak, is that from childhood I have resisted the notion of culture in Spanish. There was not another noun in my childish Spanish vocabulary that made me more uneasy than the word *"cultura"* (which was always used against me, but as indistinguishable from me—something I had betrayed). I did not shrink from culture's cousin-noun, *"costumbre"*—custom, habit—which was visible, tangible, comestible, conditional.

In Spanish, culture is indissoluble; culture is everything that connects me to the past and with a sense of myself as beyond myself. When I was a boy and refused to speak Spanish (because I spoke English), then could not speak Spanish from awkwardness, then guilt, Mexican relatives criticized my parents for letting me "lose it"—my culture, they said. (So it was possible to lose, after all? If culture is so fated, how could I have lost it?) Many years later, complete strangers—Hispanic readers and academics, even non-Hispanic readers and academics—picked up the taunting refrain. As if culture were a suitcase left too long unclaimed. I had lost my culture. The penalty for my sin was a life of inauthenticity. Then they commenced hurling coconuts—all those unchivalric taunts that are the stock of racial and sexual and patriotic bullies.

The audience is bound to misunderstand what I will tell them. There is nothing fateful about the notion of culture in American English. (The English word means exactly the opposite of the Spanish word.) The word "culture" in America comes equipped with add-on component jacks. The word "culture" in America pivots on a belief in the individual's freedom to choose, to become a person different from her past. Culture in American English separates children from grandparents, the living from the dead, this moment from what I believed only yesterday. "Culture gaps" and "culture shocks," "cultural pride" and "counterculture" are American specialties, presupposing obsolescence.

Insofar as I remain culturally influenced by Latin America, I must notice the fallacy that supports the American "I": American individualism is a communally derived value, not truly an expression of individuality. The teenager persists in rebelling against her parents, against tradition or custom, because she is shielded (blindfolded, entranced, drugged) by American culture from the knowledge that she inherited her rebellion from dead ancestors and living parents.

But insofar as I am culturally American, my gringo eye sees only diversity among the millions of people who call themselves Hispanic. The songwriter from Buenos Aires, the Bolivian from a high mountain village, the Mayan Indian who refuses Spanish, the Mayan Indian who exaggerates Spanish, the Salvadoran evangelical Protestant, the Cuban anticommunist, the Cuban communist, the green criminal, the Catholic nun, the red poet, the city dweller, the inhabitant of the desert, the swimmer from the tropics, the agnostic scientist with a German surname—Hispanics all! In no sense can so many different lives be said to inhabit a singular culture. Save one sense: Hispanics in the United States are united in the belief (a Latin American belief) that culture is a more uniform source of identity than blood.

The African-American professor has concluded his speech. He catches my eye as he sits. We smile conspiratorially. He assumes we plot the same course. Then the white journalist rises to speak. The journalist says, "Racism has not gone away, it haunts our streets, it haunts our courtrooms, it haunts our boardrooms, it haunts our classrooms . . ."

When Americans speak about "race" they remind me of Latin Americans speaking of "culture."

Culture in Latin American Spanish is fated.
Culture in American English yields to idiosyncracy.
Race in American English is fated.
Race in Latin American Spanish yields to idiosyncracy.

I hardly mean to imply racism does not exist in Latin America. Latin America predictably favors light over dark. Certainly in Mexico, the Latin American country I know best, white ascends. Certainly, the whitest dinner party I ever attended was a Mexico City dinner party where a Mexican squire of exquisite manner, mustache, and flán-like jowl, expressed himself surprised, so surprised, to learn that I am a writer. One thought he would never get over it. *Un escritor . . . ¿Un escritor . . . ?* Turning the word on a lathe of tooth and tongue, until: "You know, in Mexico, I think we do not have writers who look like you," he said. He meant dark skin, thick lips, Indian nose, bugger your mother.

No one in the United States has ever matched the confidence of that gentleman's insult. I believe it would not occur to the deepest-dyed racist in the United States to question whether I am a writer. The racist might say I look like a monkey, but he would not say I don't look like a writer.

The dream of Mexico is an apotheosis of bleach. Nevertheless, Mexico has for centuries compiled a ravishing lexicon of brown because in Mexico race is capricious as history is capricious. From the colonial era, the verbal glamour of Mexico has been to entertain a spectrum of brown—of impurity—as rich and as wet as a Hollander palette: *mestizo, castizo, alvina, chino, negro torno atras, morisco, canbujo, albarrasado, tente en el aire, canpa mulato, coyote, vorsino, lobo . . .*

By contrast, white and black discussions of race in America are Victorian; leave out the obvious part. In light of postmodern America's obsession with sex, it is remarkable how reluctant we are to sexualize American history. In an American conversation, where there is no admission of brown, the full meaning of the phrase "New World" lies always out of sight.

In eighteenth-century Mexico there was a popular genre of paintings on the subject of *las castas*—descriptive not of social caste, but of racial admixture. The paintings were illustrations of racial equations: If mama is *negra* and papa is *indio,* then baby is . . . An auxiliary convention of these paintings is that they catalog and display fruits and fauna of the New World— dogs, lizards, parrots, as well as costume, fabric. Both words and paintings describe domestic bliss or comic discord. In one panel, *la negra* is about to brain her Spanish spouse with an indigenous frying pan—à la Maggie and Jiggs—and the entire adventure and preoccupation of the New World is seen as genetic. But comically so. This, despite Latin America's fame for a tragic disposition. This, despite the fame of the United States for optimism.

In American English, mulatto traces the distance from a contaminant. In eighteenth-century Latin America, mulatto was only one pinion on a carnival wheel. In the United States of the eighteenth century, the condition of being a mulatto was an offense when it was thought to issue from black male desire. When mulatto was the issue of white male desire, mulatto was unspoken, invisible, impossible.

Brown made Americans mindful of tunnels within their bodies, about which they did not speak; about their ties to nature, about which they did not speak; about their ties to one another, about which they did not speak.

This undermining brown motif, this erotic tunnel, was the private history and making of America. Brown was the light of day. Brown, the plain evidence. Fugue and funk. Brown, the color of consort; brown, the color of illicit passion—not blue— brown, the shade of love and drawn shades and of love children, so-called, with straight hair and gothic noses; secret cousins; brown, the stench of rape and of shame, sin, slippage, birth.

After several brown centuries, I sit on a dais, in a hotel ball-room, brown. I do not hesitate to say into a microphone what everyone knows, what no one says. *Most American blacks are not black.* The erotic history of America kept pace with segregation. From the inception of America, interracial desire proceeded apace with segregated history. (The biological impulse of creatures is stronger than any cultural impulse, apparently.) Desire and sympathy, as well as cruelty and revulsion, undermined and propelled America's New World experiment from the beginning. In spite of dire social prohibitions, white slave owners placed their ancestors in the bodies of their slaves.

We know from the gossip outside books that generations before Thomas Jefferson and Sally Hemmings, black female and white male pairings existed, some lasting from youth till death did them part. But the issue of such white-black eroticism was not recognized as being brown, or both. Mulattos, quadroons, octoroons, tracing distance from the contaminant, were ultimately an irrelevance under the dictum of the American racial theory called the "one-drop" theory.

In the American musical *Showboat,* a backwater sheriff boards the *Cotton Blossom,* or whatever that showboat was called, to declaim, in cadences of Racine (and to make himself plain to the second balcony), *One drop o' nigger blood 'sall it takes . . .*

To make a nigger. Here was an anthropology, a biology, indeed an alchemy, that allowed plantation owners to protect their investment, to preserve the assumption of racial superiority, to accommodate, as well, their sexual curiosity and to redouble their chattel.

A child of black-and-white eroticism remained "black" in the light of day, no matter how light her skin, straight his hair, gothic her nose; she was black as midnight, black as tar, black as the ace of spades, black as your hat. Under the one-drop theorem, it was possible for a white mother to give birth to a black child in America, but no black mother ever gave birth to a white child. A New World paradox.

One of the first lessons in America, the color-book lesson, instructs that color should stay within the lines. The river should not flood its banks. The tree should not smear the sky.

It is interesting to note the two American fictions of the nineteenth century that continue to romance us were about interracial relationships, exclusively male. I mean *The Adventures of Huckleberry Finn* and *Moby-Dick*—both dreams of escape from convention and family. At a time when America was preoccupied with land and settlement, with cultivating the land, Twain and Melville wrote of water, of suspension, of being carried outward. The river cares nothing for its bank, the ocean cares nothing for the shore, each consorts with the sky. In the first, a white boy and a runaway slave abandon town and the constriction of the shore for the freedom of the river. In the latter, a crew of men from every corner of the world board a ship in search of a ghostly whale. In both stories there are only undomesticated men or boys. And the male pairings are odd, interracial, even homoerotic; violations of the town's conventions.

After the Civil War, in American places where water seduced or penetrated the landscape, the promiscuity of the horizon encouraged African Americans who lived near those places to speak the truth about themselves. In New Orleans and

Charleston, African Americans often described themselves as "Creoles" or "mulattos"—washes, watercolors—some Latin influence, perhaps. But the landlocked places kept to the shackle of blood-as-fate; color within the lines.

The notion that a brown is black—a paucity of choice—created segregated drinking fountains and schoolrooms and colored platoons in the Second World War. But that same notion—the one-drop notion—also undermined segregation in America by forging a solidarity among African Americans over and above any extenuations such as occupation or age or income or complexion.

▪ ▪ ▪

My friend Darrell. Darrell says he is black. Darrell says he is black because *that is what the white cop sees when he looks at me.*

If it is fair for me to notice that the white Latina at Yale is not objectively a person of color, is it fair to notice you are not exactly black? Darrell?

You know what I'm talking about . . .

Of course I understand what you're talking about. Race is the sine qua non among American transactions. Without race, we wouldn't have music, movies, prisons, politics, history, libraries, colleges, private conversations, motives. Dorothy Dandridge. Bill Clinton. Race is America's theme—not freedom, not democracy (as we say in company). What are you? we say. Well, we don't say anymore, but we mean. And you say black.

What do you say?

I don't.

Yes you do. You say, queer Indian Catholic—some sidestep bullshit like that.

I don't say brown. Anyway, how should I know what race I am, my ancestors go back a long way. I grant you, were it not for America's preoccupation with distinguishing feathers, I would have to learn a trade other than brown. To be a warbler is not the same as being a brown warbler.

Speaking of warblers. I saw a blackbird the other day—Avian-American—he was sitting in the sun. Little patch of lawn. In this particular sun—or was it just the Fabergé of the moment?—the blackbird appeared green, green as ink, and with gold tracery upon the nib of his folded wing; the green of the grayest recesses of the swooniest forest of Fragonard.

Blackbirds are green,
Violets blue . . . So?

So, I believe I do not truly understand you, Darrell, your resort to imprecision to color yourself from another's regard. Maybe because I have never been taken, mistaken, though I do get stopped often enough by cops for jogging in my white-out neighborhood. Do you believe you uphold the one-drop theory by your insistence on black, because that is the way the white cop sees you?

Too easy, Rodriguez.

It doesn't matter if my complexion is lemon or redbone or licorice, I'm black—the word that drips down indelible as India ink through the language because black is incapable of qualification. You can have black and blue. You can have black and white. You can have The Red and the Black. *But you can't have reddish black or light black or blackish, as you have reddish brown. Black is historically dense because it is linguistically dense; it overwhelms any more complicated shading. You can say I'm self-consciously black. You want to say that instead of black? That's my race. Self-Conscious. I dream about an unself-conscious gesture or moment or thought. Or step. An unself-conscious boulevard. Or fellowship. I won't find it. Not in Harlem. Not in Paris. Not in Oakland on Easter Sunday morning. There's always a split-second delay between you and me—a linguistic felt-tip line. I am the line in the color book! Is my fly open? Am I scaring somebody? Is your tone ironic or condescending? Is there a third choice? No, I don't believe there is a third choice. I can detect the slightest tremor of misgiving faster than Jane Austen. Sensibility, she called her faculty, and that's what black folk are masters of—sensibility. My eyes are two-way mirrors. My deliberation is reflexive. Because my hue cannot reflect? What do they think of me? And speaking of mirrors: Mirror, mirror on the wall, does this outfit look too spooky? Too out there? Rap stars and kids can get away with an out-law look, as you call it, but a black man better stick with* Lands' End. *When I say I'm black-because-that's-what-the-white-cop-sees, I mean I'm a man of sensibility. Buck is the thinnest skin there is, babe. Absorbs everything.*

Uphold the one-drop theory? Come on! I don't make this stuff up, you know. And if you'll kindly advise the San Fran-

*cisco Police Department their way of thinking is recherché,
I'll be much obliged and I'll call myself something else.*

▪ ▪ ▪

What of white, then? White flesh is reductive. Caucasian is a
term of no scientific currency. White is an impulse to remain
innocent of history.

For many generations, the American paint box was predicated upon an unsullied white, an irreducible, an unblushing,
a bloodless white—let us say, cadmium—let us say, rather, the
white of the powder on George Washington's head; let us say,
rather, the white of the driven snow, for the first white Americans imagined themselves innocent. And white is universally
accepted, among white people, as the color of innocence.

It is impossible to depict or portray white in time—even the
white of philosophy, even the white of an hour—without a
complex palette. (Though Japanese painting portrays white—
the cloud obscuring a mountaintop or the mist in a valley—
as an absence of paint.) Fra Angelico's *Transfiguration* might
serve us here. Christ's transfigured robes are described in
Scripture as whiter than any bleach could make them. In order
to paint (rather than to absent) a supernaturally irradiated garment, a garment outside time, Fra Angelico must call upon
time—drape and shadow—and, in so doing, must call upon
pigment, literally mortal clay, yellow and red and gray and
brown and black. Later, we see, Christ used dirt and spit as a
healing paste; a mixture to restore sight.

Brown marks the passage of time.

▪ ▪ ▪

After a speech or a panel discussion like the one I here rehearse, someone from the audience will approach me, "someone who is white," she says. She feels she has no culture. She envies me. She envies what I have been at pains to escape—the Mexican sense of culture.

The price of entering white America is an acid bath, a bleaching bath—a transfiguration—that burns away memory. I mean the freedom to become; I mean the freedom to imagine oneself free.

The point of Noel Ignatiev's *How the Irish Became White* (by distancing themselves from black) may be extended to any number of other European immigrants to America. *How the Germans became white. How Sicilian Catholics became white. How Russian Jews became white.*

Extended even to non-Europeans: *How my mother and father became white.* My Mexican parents were described as White on their citizenship papers by an unimaginative federal agent. (An honorary degree.)

Who can blame the Irish steward or the Sicilian hatmaker for wanting to be white? White in America was the freedom to disappear from a crowded tenement and to reappear in a Long Island suburb, in an all-electric kitchen, with a set of matching plates.

I grew up wanting to be white. That is, to the extent of wanting to be colorless and to feel complete freedom of movement. The other night at a neighborhood restaurant the waiter, after mentioning he had read my books, said about himself, "I'm white, I'm nothing." But that was what I wanted, you see, growing up in America—the freedom of being nothing, the confidence of it, the arrogance. And I achieved it.

Growing up an honorary white—which meant only that I was not black—I never wanted to be black, like the white kids wanted to be black (Elvis Presley wanting to be black), such was their white freedom! White, which began as an idea of no color; which defined itself against black and was therefore always bordered with black; white in America ended up as freedom from color—an idea of no boundary. Call me Ishmael.

Whereas whites regarded their Americanization as a freedom from culture, black was fated because black was blood. Blood was essence; black was essence. *Yo, blood!* If you are black, to this day, if you are young, black, you can end up with siblings, classmates, who will challenge you for speaking "white," thinking "white," even though every white kid assumes the right to sing black and talk black and move black. So "black," once a restriction imposed by whites in defiance of obvious history, black now is a culture (in the fated sense) imposed by blacks.

Within their restriction, using restriction subversively, using whatever was not valued by the ugly stepsisters (using poverty, bruise, prayer), African Americans created the most vibrant culture of America, now the defining culture of America. White Americans would end up feeling themselves bloodless. White Americans would end up hungering for black culture, which they understood curiously as freedom of expression, glamour of transcendence.

To make black culture, so the American myth goes, one needs to connect to misery; one needs to be bad or battered to sing the blues. How many millions of African Americans today need to rot in jail cells to maintain the culture of partition, to keep black culture outlaw, to keep outlaw black culture at the center of white yearning?

What I want for African Americans is white freedom. The same as I wanted for myself.

The last white freedom in America will be the freedom of the African American to admit brown. Miscegenation. To speak freely of ancestors, of Indian and Scots and German and plantation owner. To speak the truth of themselves. That is the great advantage I can see for blacks in the rise of the so-called Hispanic.

What Latin America might give the United States is a playful notion of race. Already the definitive blond in America is Tina Turner.

What the United States might give Latin America is a more playful notion of culture. Culture as freedom. Culture as invitation. Culture as lure. Already, the definitive blond in Latin America is Ricky Martin. Ricky Martin is so blond he can afford to be brunette.

Only further confusion can save us. My favorite San Francisco couple is a Chinese-American man and an African-American woman who both have blond hair and wear Hawaiian shirts and ride around town in a vintage red Pontiac convertible with white leather upholstery. The use of vegetable hair dyes is a great boon to American youth, wouldn't you say? Such wonderfully false colors allow young Americans to be and not to be. Blue or chartreuse or Lucille Ball. And at the same time to proclaim themselves to be just kidding. And contact lenses. My niece has dyed her hair red and thinks she might like to try blue eyes for a change. Nothing permanent. It all washes out. Tomorrow and tomorrow and tomorrow.

Ding-dong. It's the UPS man. The Filipino guy in shorts, his hair just beginning to magenta at the temples. Home, as I said, is a Victorian in San Francisco with Indians stomping around on the roof. And I am left (on such a nice day, too) sitting inside, deconstructing the American English word for myself—Hispanic [*sic*]—by which I celebrate my own deliverance from *cultura;* the deliverance of the United States of America from race.

- *Chapter Seven* •

DREAMS OF A
TEMPERATE PEOPLE

WOULD YOU RATHER FREEZE TO DEATH OR DIE IN A DESERT?
Not such an odd question if you knew my father, if you understood Mexico. (All abstraction like all humor in Mexico
presupposes a corpse.) We were driving that day toward a Mexican market on the Yolo County side of the Sacramento River.
The car windows were rolled down to admit the blast of summer heat, which, in conjunction with the approaching minaret
of a Foster's Freeze, occasioned my father's question.

I have lived most of my life within a hundred miles of that
question. However theatrically I pose myself, I remain a temperate man. I have questioned the torrid zone. I have no experience of it, of a life given over to passion, I mean. The lush,
yes. I have experimented with luxe, with hotels that pretend to
other centuries (have noticed, lately, how they aspire to naught,
to some austerity of boredom or flight).

Thomas Carew, seventeenth-century English poet, wit, courtier:

Give me more love, or more disdain;
The torrid or the frozen zone
Bring equal ease unto my pain;
The temperate affords me none.

It is only in middle age I deliberate the thermodynamic quatrain. I remember Colette's first glimpse of the passionate zone. (I remember reading this passage at a laundromat, at approximately the same age at which Colette portrays herself.) Colette as a young woman did not know passion existed outside of books. She had married a middle-aged man. One night she was awakened by her husband, who asked her to accompany him to intervene in a lovers' quarrel—some acquaintances of his, theatricals. Later, having appeased the passionate couple, and on their way home:

> *"Are you cold? You don't want to go home on foot, do you?"* (The husband.)
> *No, I was not cold. Yes, I was cold. All the same, I would have liked to go home on foot. Or not to go home at all. Walking beside him, I looked back in my mind at the room we had just left. I can see something of it still—highlights of pale blue against a dim background . . . the tumbled, white expanse of a lovers' bed.*

However little contemplation I have given to lovers' beds, I know something of heat, having been raised in California's Central Valley. A favorite pastime of valley children was to imagine winter while in the throes of summer. (As easily as children feign sleep or death in games.) There was room for imagination; we were never wedded to the sun, like those men and women who toil over this terrible earth, heads downcast, as in the silvered paintings of Corot. Sitting outside on a summer day, sucking on ice cubes held in paper napkins, my brother and sisters and I would conjure ice and fog and wind; I would place an ice cube at the first vertebra of my sister's back and demand: *Are you cold?*

I became a voracious reader; I was ambitious for an intellectual life I imagined belonging only to towers, gray cities, winter—to monks in cold cells, poets in scarves, women in furs, Edmund Wilson. On warm summer evenings, sitting outside, I read drafty nineteenth-century novels wherein inn signs creaked on their hinges and bare branches tapped against windowpanes.

I am even less familiar with cold than with passion. I did not see falling snow until I was twenty-three years old. I was, at the moment of my epiphany, a graduate student at Columbia University; I was sitting beside a tall window, in a lecture hall that resembled a violin; a lecture on Hegel that resembled a violin. The light queered. The sky turned to pewter, "gunmetal gray," as in books. My mouth opened. Only then, snow.

■ ■ ■

For the greater part of my life my address has been within walking distance of the Pacific, within a climate fabled for mildness. Here in San Francisco, outside my window, bright or not, it is usually late March, early spring. Days in August one must wear a sweater of some sort; days in January one walks about in shirtsleeves. As I am writing these words, it is the darling month, and yet a fire burns in the grate.

Jack London was born on the other side of San Francisco, over on Third Street. South. If there is any sun today, it is there, where pale colonizers of cyberspace work long hours to pare time from a world of theoretically unlimited space, but of no weather. Jack London seems to me a true native son insofar as he, too, grew up preoccupied by extremes of weather; invented animate climates far distant.

London wrote stories of white men shanghaied off the Embarcadero, drugged in the holds of ships, then awakening to tropical winds in black sails. Or, in London's famous story of cold, "To Build a Fire," cold pursues the solitary hero through the dark. The hero stumbles, falls, his clothes freeze to his body. Then cold grips him as an enchantress might: "Freezing was not so bad as people thought . . . the most comfortable and satisfying sleep he had ever known."

The story seemed to come from the other side of the moon to a boy shivering on his summer porch. The same boy had seen gringos (women or Robert Morley types, fat, effete) crossing the desert in movies at the air-conditioned Tower Theater; they often nodded off on their camels and had to be slapped back to life by savvy brown hands. *You muzz not to zleep in ze dezert.* So we are to understand that heat is as deadly as ice; perhaps as comfortable.

Transposed Easterners tell me they will never feel comfortable or "at home" in coastal California because they miss the seasons. They say this as if they are intoning Ecclesiastes. Even without such disapproval, a suspicion has troubled native Californians. That we risk childishness. That we live oblivious to some knowledge of good and evil. That we will never know what Edmund Wilson knew. *What did Edmund Wilson know?* (A woman from Boston lived for several years in Rio de Janeiro. Her summation: "These are not serious people.")

The darkest fiction coastal California has produced is confounded by a cloudless sky. In the California detective novel, the corpse is sprawled upon the linoleum of a weekly hotel, the sun pours aslant onto the floor, lengthens into afternoon, slowly contracts to midnight. Nor does the inn sign creak. It blinks.

▪ ▪ ▪

In *Arctic Dreams,* Barry Lopez observes Americans "as temperate zone people . . . have long been ill-disposed toward deserts and expanses of tundra and ice."

However fierce is America's history, however notorious we are for the violence of our impulse, the prevailing myth of Americans (among ourselves) is indeed temperate. We prefer plainness in our theology, in our food, in our rhetoric; we mistrust extremes of allegiance; we mistrust even excessive plainness. Thus, too, did we construct caution into our system of governance—three countervailing powers to keep any one office or person or kind from holding too much. America is strong, we believe, because the majority belongs to the middle class, the temperate class; strangers alike to extremes of wealth and want.

Foreigners point to our Civil War as evidence of internecine hotness.

Silently we refer foreigners to cool marble monuments dedicated to young Americans sent to fight in foreign lands where the tyrants of winter held sway.

Foreigners point to our Wild West.

But foreigners misunderstand the early American's sense of his task. The impulse of the Wild West was not wildness but domesticity.

In cowboy movies at the air-conditioned Tower Theater, the Wild West was a province of lost boys: an assay office and a saloon, presided over by the only suit in town, Blackie—Mister Blackie—who sported a close-clipped mustache and a string tie, who smoked cigars, but not the big kind. Until: One particularly fine morning, the second wave of newcomers arrives—the temperate wave, the civilizers—the schoolteacher and the preacher, Starbucks, Aaron Copeland, Laura Ingalls Wilder, and the new sheriff, ardent, book-learned, loose-forelocked.

Caught in the middle—linking the generation of disorder to incoming good—stands the theatrical moll, the prostitute, saloon singer, a pragmatist who has an "arrangement" with Blackie (she lives upstairs in his saloon), though she reserves a transparently good heart and reveals a foreshadowing bullet-hole-sized beauty mark on her powdered left breast. She comes quickly to more than admire the sheriff, who says to her, "I'll bet you'd look real pretty without all that war paint." In the face of such naïveté, she must lower her spidery lashes. We understand she will never live to wear gingham. The schoolmistress, who doesn't put out, will get the sheriff.

Beyond the muddy edges of town, there was never any question about the horizon's meaning. The horizon was an encroaching wilderness, unmaking. *Blackboard Jungle. Dragnet. The Man with the Golden Arm. The War of the Worlds. Frankenstein. Psycho.* The barely inhabited West was where sociopaths roamed, where Gabby Hayes minced around in an apron, and mountain men bedded doe-eyed Indian maidens who had hearts of wampum, but would never live to wear-um gingham. The confrontation with wildness was the coming attraction, more of the same. Onward, onward would the pioneers move—westward—west toward Burbank.

Hollywood began putting the brakes on cowboy movies in the late fifties; Burbank was enveloped by smog.

■　■　■

In the 1930s, that quintessential New Yorker, Edmund Wilson, took his chilly brain on tour. He discovered here, in the Far West—in temperate San Diego—the highest number of suicides in the country; the highest rate of depression. "You seem to see the last futile effervescence of the burst of the American adventure. Here our people, so long told to 'go West' to escape from ill health and poverty, maladjustment and industrial oppression, are discovering that, having come West, their problems and diseases remain and that the ocean bars further flight."

What Edmund Wilson knew would not yet alter the nation's sense of the land and its meaning. Throughout the twentieth century, as throughout the nineteenth, Americans were famously an east-west people. We told our meaning as we told time, counterclockwise. The past lay east, the future west. Europe, the previous shore, was the Old World; we the new, the ringing moment, twelve o'clock. China, the old again, and so on.

Some Americans once took fatal exception to the east-west narrative line. Civil War rebels invented a south-north point of view, insisting that Easterners were in fact Northerners. Beyond the slave owner's sin, the impertinence committed by Southerners was their invention of a heterodox narrative line.

The Mexican novelist Carlos Fuentes once described the Mason-Dixon line as the border to Latin America. Perhaps Fuentes meant that the Old South, like the Latin South, was a culture agrarian in its ethos, baroque in its social organization; so actual in its imaginative life as to appear fantastic. Flannery O'Conner, Eudora Welty, as magical realists. And Faulkner, of course (according to García Márquez).

In *Walden,* Henry David Thoreau extolled the wild goose as "more of a cosmopolite than we"—we Americans. "He breaks his fast in Canada, takes a luncheon in the Ohio, and plumes himself for the night in a southern bayou." The advantage of the Canadian goose, in Thoreau's exemplum, is that Nature obliges geese to a north-south runnel.

Thoreau was determined to take the direction of his life from Nature. But Nature, as manifest in the purlieus of Walden Pond, was not the Nature of the Wild West. Wild-eyed teenagers who left Concord for Sacramento were of a different, an adversarial, opinion regarding Nature. Thoreau was horrified by stories of the cruelty toward Nature of westering Americans— accounts of a giant redwood cut down; photographs of young men dancing upon the sawn stump. America would never have achieved temperance if westering Americans' estimate of Nature had not been so mad; if America's reverence for domesticity had not been so mad.

The mid-twentieth century brought federal discontinuity to the American narrative line. The U.S. Congress brought geographical exotics—Hawaii and Alaska—two new "states" into our union. Both territories were exteriors—anti-domestic in theme, in aspect. The one forbidding, the other erotic; both compositions of water—the one frozen, the other melted sky.

By the early 1960s, popular technologies like cheap air conditioners and jet airplanes, plastic cups and Interstates, reoriented Americans upon new migratory paths and new spiritual paths. Popular technologies ameliorated the tension of the east-west line, which was also the Judeo-Christian line, which was also the transcontinental railroad.

Americans, for the first time, were released from the tyranny of seasons, as well as from the sympathy of seasons, as well as from any defining sense of rootedness. The country divided, in popular speech, in fashion, in fiction, into zones of cold and hot. The "rust belt" became our corrupting past—the end of the Industrial Age. The Sun Belt was a newer, more ancient history that intrigued; a zone of preference. The Sun Belt adapted folkways of Native American spirituality. The Sun Belt was at once the launching pad for modern missiles—a new age of exploration—and a prehistoric landing strip.

The artificial breeze (popular technologies like cheap air conditioners and jet planes) lured Americans from the temperate zone, to situate a new majority of the nation within a bright

Gehenna. Though they were following the trail of Thoreau's Canadian goose southward, the jet stream pioneers were no less determined than their westering ancestors to govern Nature. The Sun Belt thermostat was fixed; it went no higher, no lower, than spring. People of the New South claimed not to feel the heat; people claimed not to think about heat because they were piped, from the air-conditioned office building to the air-conditioned car; from the car to the front door. In between, the merest intimation of an intemperate Nature.

Today's Michigan matron, let us say, and despite her arthritis, for which there is no cure, and despite chronic disappointment, for which there is no cure, nevertheless flies with the complacency of Thoreau's goose. At the first sign of frost, she abandons her native thirty-two degrees for a two-hours-distant condo on a fake lagoon in Florida that used to be a lagoon. The Michigan matron, let us say, now imagines America as she imagines her life, as she imagines her garden—as bounded by seasonal borders. Between airports there is no sense of direction. There is Departure and there is Arrival. Exit autumn; enter spring. In between there is only a manageable interval of stale air.

■ ■ ■

Easterners and Midwesterners who moved south into the Sun Belt found themselves living alongside Hispanics whose habit was to describe the United States as *"el norte,"* describing their journey. That description became my father's habit as well—California as *el norte*—though my father's impulse was ironic and was meant, as were most of my father's utterances, to mark my father's distance from American perspective. *El norte* became my father's gloss on the gringo's sense of history, the gringo's compass, but also the Mexican grudge, but also the Mexican infantilism (clinging to Mother Mexico), but also my father's disappointment with his own placement in the world. But also his son's optimism (my inclination to be buoyed by the weightless optimism of the West). I had no history. I was born in the West.

One morning my father announced: "We came north to live in the American West, Mama," as if this were the script for an American movie about our family. My mother was oblivious of the joke, which was directed, anyway, at my ambition. For, you see, my father understood my ambition. My father had no past in Mexico. He had been an orphan. He left Mexico as one leaves a cold room.

My family knew many Mexican men who came to *el norte* only to work. They came north in order to sustain the dream of a complete and enduring life elsewhere. Never did these Mexican men speak of having left the past behind, as Westerners in Sacramento spoke of having left the past behind them, or as my father spoke of the past as beneath him. These Mexican men worked to sustain the past; they sent money to the past every Saturday. From the Mexican migrants' point of view, California was a commute.

The Mexican ambition for *el norte* has changed since my childhood, insofar as it has become a predominantly metropolitan ambition. Most peasants who now travel north follow rumors of cities of gold, where there are dishes that need washing, beds that need making, roofs that need mending, swimming pools that need cleaning. From the Mexican migrants' point of view, *el norte* remains a robust ambition, a robust way of looking at the American West. *El norte* remains a viable term.

At academic conferences on the American West (*Whither the American West?*), I now find myself auditing the proceeding with something of my father's sensibility, something of his humor. Professors in cowboy boots speak of the fragility of the American West. The future is a danger to the American West, no longer its point. Ecologists, historians, call for intervention; speak of Indians needing protection (not the gambling tribes); they speak of streams, trees, salmon, wetlands—wilderness—as needing protection.

What is endangered in America is the notion of the West.

In the late 1950s, at the same time that California became the most populous state, Alaska became a new horizon—an albino hope, a gray-rolled cumulus, a glacial obsession—like Melville's great whale. Alaska absorbed all the nouns that lay bleaching along the Oregon Trail. Solitude. Vacancy. Wilderness.

Several states now cluster under the white belly of Alaska: Idaho, Wyoming, Montana, Washington, Oregon, northern portions of Colorado and Utah. In something like the way the East Coast invented the West, California has invented a rectified North. From the perspective of California, Oregon is a northern state; Seattle is a northern city. Vancouver becomes a part of the continuum without regard to international borders.

Many Americans already need an escape from the overpopulated cities of the sun. The new North is where environmentalists seek a purer air or stream, a less crowded freeway. The disenchanted seek simplicity. The new North is where militiamen seek an older, whiter, elbow-roomier America. The new North is where nostalgic skinheads pursue the Norman Rockwell idyll, fleeing Hispanics who swarm the construction sites in L.A.

In the new nation of *el norte,* where we are all destined to live, the limits of our anthem will no longer be from sea to shining sea, as in the Katharine Lee Bates lyric. A newer America opens to extremes of weather and landscape and discontent—hot and cold—as in the Irving Berlin lyric: Dreaming of snow in Beverly Hills.

■ ■ ■

The dilemma of California remains as Edmund Wilson described it. We have built right up to the edge of the sea. It is also that the soil and the air promote contesting legends. The earth in California is finite, animate, unreliable—the earth quakes, burns, slides into the sea. The tiniest houses cost a million dollars. But the air is temperate—light and vast—a stepping-off place, and we have only recently discovered how.

Even as I write, American migratory paths are digitally scrambling. The Internet is everywhere advertised as an advance to equal the opening of the Northwest Territory or the transcontinental railway. American business is in a frenzy to leave the earth, following restless Californian imagination "on-line."

California has found an aperture, which is not up or down or sideways but rather is a race without a goal, an application without a purpose; speed without distance; infinitude without place. A revolution—yes, everyone agrees it is a revolution—without a point.

For purposes of this book, the digital divide is between the Few and the Many. The Few will continue to disport themselves within their exception, as is their custom. For purposes of this book, the Many are many more than they were. They sleep in shanties. They shit in holes. They give birth from their bodies, incorrigibly. They move in real time upon the real surface of the earth. They are moving from South to North.

▪ ▪ ▪

When Canada, Mexico, and the United States signed the North American Free Trade Agreement, the Canadian and the Mexican politely acknowledged each other, as rumors sometimes do upon meeting. *Haut* shook hands with *Sur*. A vertical alignment, yes, but Nafta signified more than a meeting of basement and balcony. The surprise was mezzo. President William Jefferson Clinton rose to welcome Canada and Mexico into "the American future"—words blazing like northern lights on an Eskimo Pie packet.

The American imagination—that is, the U.S. imagination—stood to change most by the agreement. The American future, which had always lain westward, was rhetorically recalibrated that day to north and south. Henceforward, the American future will not be reckoned a sunrise; decline will not be reckoned a sunset. We will need a vocabulary appropriate to people of the middle.

When Canada, Mexico, and the United States signed the North American Free Trade Agreement, I was reminded of Thoreau's recommended cosmopolitanism, an antidote to the New York provincialism that daily rankles. I was as quickly reminded of Octavio Paz and Marshall McLuhan.

Canada and Mexico have produced North American intellectuals a generation ahead of the United States. U.S. intellectuals of the middleweight New York school continue to uphold the east-to-west custom of intellectual property in order to maintain their authority as critics. East Coast intellectuals continue to contest with the Old World, especially the notorious tag team of England and France.

Mexico and Canada are alike north-south countries. In Mexican history, marauding hordes descend upon the capital from the North. Mexican mothers fear losing their children to jobs in the North. The Mexican North is little distinct from the United States, whereas the South in Mexico reassures; stones of Indian civilization litter the jungle floor.

Octavio Paz, the greatest writer of his Mexican generation, wrote of the larger world as only someone not born at the center of any map can. Paz wrote of Hindu spirituality, French painting, Yankee pot roast. Paz lived for a time in the United States and returned frequently in his writing to the dialectic posed by the proximity of the United States and Mexico—their shared difference.

In Canada, the North represents continuity, the unchanging aspect of the nation. Old-timers in autumn speak of the winter as the North—the North is coming, they say. Whereas the Canadian south is little distinct from the United States.

Marshall McLuhan is as distinct from Paz as is wit from romance. McLuhan is the other writer of the last century whose work seems to me comparably North American. A scholar of Renaissance rhetoric at the University of Toronto, McLuhan employed antinomy to decode new technologies that would shorten the attention span of the postwar world. McLuhan read the future as he would read an arcane text. McLuhan lived close enough to the American boom box to suffer its concussion; far enough removed to consider objectively the effect of American culture on civilization. And incidentally, to regret. In his stoic regard of a future he found deplorable, McLuhan never asked (as Mexico invariably will ask) why things have to go the American way. His thesis is plain: Things will.

It was Octavio Paz's vanity, as a Mexican of the old school, to assume his nation's cultural imperishability. He could not have anticipated, so soon after his death, that Mexico would elect a Coca-Cola cowboy to the presidency, a president who would express in English his wish for a borderless future.

Even after Nafta, Paz continued to refer to citizens of the United States as *"norteamericanos,"* an old Mexican habit. But, of course, the Mexican is as much a *norteamericano* as the gringo is—more so, I think, since so many Mexican peasants commute up and down, as easy with one version of themselves as with another. What that might mean for Mexico's notion of an unchanging South, Paz never let himself imagine before he turned into a postage stamp.

If history is male, as Octavio Paz was male—as intractable, I mean—then power, influence, conquest belongs only to the stronger contestant. One buck vanquishes all other currency.

Farewell, old Paz. Mexicans drink more Coca-Cola than Americans drink.

President Vicente Fox is the first Americanized president of Mexico. President George W. Bush is America's first Hispanic president. And Canada is already brown. Vancouver has become an Anglo-Chinese city, for example. What if history is female, and as permeable as McLuhan's eye and ear? Marshall McLuhan observed the moment America's culture becomes the culture of the world it is no longer American culture. What if victory can sometimes belong to the nation or people who most readily absorb a foreign culture? Capitalism flourishes in Vietnam. The elegancies of the English language are formidably sustained by Jane Austens in Sri Lanka. The Japanese stole the manufacture of the automobile from Detroit, because the Japanese were preoccupied with refining what they admired. If history is male, there is no way to understand such subversions.

▪ ▪ ▪

Canada has never been much of an idea for Americans. We like Canada. Our good neighbor. Never hear them. Tidy.

Downstairs . . . well, so many people come and go. What can they be up to? Mexico is a brown idea we would rather not discuss.

To the extent Americans wish to believe ourselves a people of temperance, Canada disturbs us. Canada is more orderly than we Americans know ourselves to be.

It interests Americans that Canada is clean and empty and unimplicating; the largest country in the world that doesn't exist. Without distinct music or food or capacity for rudeness—

less rich, less angry, less complicated, less neurotic, less dark, less brilliant. Canadians live among us rather as spies do. They are ideologically at some remove from complete compliance with us as regards the American adventure. And yet they are indistinguishable (by us) from us. Whereas Mexicans are so easily distinguishable, we think. We do not always, in speech, distinguish Mexican Americans from Mexicans.

On my way in from the airport, the Toronto cabbie was too discreet to ask outright about my face. He tried by indirection to reconcile my—Arab?—features with the academic American accent. My answer to his tentative "Which flight did you take?" evidently did not satisfy. (New York.) Emboldened, then: "Is that where you live?" (No.) Finally: "Where *do* you live?" (California.) At which point, he safely commenced a disquisition about guns and the psychological disorder south of the border. (The headline in the morning's *Globe and Mail* described mass murder at a U.S. high school.) And yet he must wonder (blue eyes filled the rearview mirror): Does wildness rise?

■ ■ ■

American politicians, American classrooms turn to Canada for an idea of orderly civic life. The saving idea is called "multiculturalism." Multiculturalism became Canadian policy in 1971 when Prime Minister Pierre Elliott Trudeau's government elaborated a solution for French Canada's coexistence within the English-speaking union.

Multiculturalism is honorable to the extent it welcomes the newcomer and mediates a monotonous Anglo-Saxon model of Canadianness. In Canada-after-Trudeau, one can be Chinese and fully Canadian. One can be Pakistani or Greek. Canada will respect the fact that *You are not I. You who are different shall be welcomed into the idea of the whole without suffering the loss of your exception.* Curiously, however, not a few brown immigrant children in today's Canada regard multiculturalism as implausible. After all, Canada is real weather and landscape and a distinct set of ideas and hotcakes and values—one of the values being the value of diversity. Canadian multiculturalism, in other words, is not "multi" at all, but culturally biased to the degree that it expresses a Canadian respect for individualism not shared by most countries in the world.

To borrow from Professor McLuhan, multiculturalism is cool. Too cool. The favored metaphor of multicultural Canada, the "mosaic"—separate units; composite by satellite—propounds a most unerotic notion of society. *You* will never inextricably entwine with *I*. Croatian and Pakistani will not graft a varietal. Montreal, once an erotic city of jazz and mix, has become the noun-splitting capital of the world. Eyes remain suspicious, tongues are held in check. French-language police in rubber soles patrol the streets, writing tickets for bilingual menus and shop signs.

With some regularity I hear from CBC radio or television (the French service in Montreal). The question is always the same: *Are Hispanics in the Southwest destined to forge some sort of new Quebec?*

Nope, madame. And here's why: Though Hispanics, particularly Chicanos in the Southwest—the noisiest among us—made their reputations "against" assimilation, Hispanics nevertheless trust most the ancient Spanish pronoun, the first-person plural pronoun, the love-potion pronoun—*nosotros*. We. Try as we will to be culturally aggrieved by day, we find the gringos kind of attractive in the moonlight.

From Radio CBC, this is dedicated to the one I love: Mexico, whence the majority of America's Hispanics derive, has no idea of anything that might resemble Canadian multiculturalism. Mexico is only learning the meaning of eighteenth-century individualism. Mexico is cruel toward her indigenous peasants in Chiapas, because Mexico is distrustful of a separate claim. Mexico speaks of her many as mix—the *mestizaje*—the marriage of races. Whereas Canada dispenses an equal prophylaxis for Syrian and Sikh, Mexico's appetite for genetic novelty is omnivorous. No one is safe when Mexico comes into heat.

Confronted by a steaming pile of runny, red-hot Mexican inevitability and a bottle of clear, cool Canadian exceptionalism, what's the American to do? In the American classroom, we preach the Canadian gospel of cultural relativism until every head nods with boredom: *Celebrate diversity. Unity through diversity. Mahala. Yo!* But after school we become more like Mexicans: The Filipina flirts with the African American. Difference is danger; danger is sexy. And America seeks a midsummer night's dream resolution to all civic dilemma.

▪ ▪ ▪

Bookstores display the American appetite for a new kind of travel book not concerned with exotic locale or contretemps, but with the unknowable, with Olympian awe—mountains, seas, furious storms, acts of God. At the end of a westering era, whereby we sought to control Nature, readers now seek to know how fragile we are, how small we are, how little we matter.

Just at the moment, American imagination is more intrigued with cold than with hot, with Ernest Shackleton than with Lawrence of Arabia (five books last year on Shackleton). Though both adventures lie south, one is cold and one is hot. The South, as mythology, is not so neatly borne out by the facts. The South, as mythology, is insupportable. Though the South Pole is ice, the South remains hot in popular imagination. South remains bottom. Gravity dictates things must fall from top to bottom, from high to low. Water runs down, sinners fall, the nude descends the staircase and is not cold, presumably, though heat rises, as we shall see.

Perhaps Americans will be rescued by the South. The South may be the region of leisure and retirement, even regeneration (a Protestant Reformation is forming in Latin America); the South is also the climate of the inevitable—the cant and the tow are inevitable. Down, down, to the netherworld of biology, sex, hair, infection, blackened skin, multiplicity, as of grains of sand. But also of faith. Abrahamic religions, religions we call "Western" are, in truth, oriental and connect us to the desert, which is southerly in our gothic imaginations. It was there Yahweh pitched His tent; lured His beloved there.

The gardener in my neighborhood (I never knew his name), a friendly jut of his chin over the whine of his leaf blower was all I knew of him. His van filled with shovels and rakes was found in the desert. His body lay some distance away. Volute, like a shell.

Another man, the man who lives around the corner, modest, tall, his eyes bent toward some concavity of the sidewalk, passes in front of my building on many afternoons. I've heard this man has been up and down Everest several times. Whenever I see him, dressed in his business suit, I feel I must—like a Victorian shopkeeper, a chemist or greengrocer—I feel I must rush out to the High Street, approach the ultramontane hero: *Please, sir, what is it like? What is Nature? What is intemperance? What does Nature intend?*

The famous nineteenth-century explorers were British, traveling to the far edges of Empire to extend Empire; making of Queen Victoria, that homely woman sitting by her fire, a symbol of the Age of Adventure. By comparison, nineteenth-century America was also a nation of travelers, not in the same dictionary sense. Most American travelers were exploring in order to settle. They were looking for home; making of that wild man Daniel Boone a symbol of the search for domesticity.

Home, ancestors, marriages made in heaven, mama, papa, family trees, monuments are vertical thoughts. Old men's thoughts. My father would often jerk his thumb upward to indicate where he was headed next—that eager, maddish smile of his, the eagerness of the Mexican boy headed north.

Americans exchange baseball and football for "extreme sports"—in which I include reckless driving, day-trading, unprotected sex, and high school massacres—whereby one's contest is with one's own body, one's nerve, one's solitude, one's fear. Death keeps score.

In *Arctic Dreams,* Barry Lopez observes Americans "as temperate zone people have long been ill-disposed toward deserts and expanses of tundra and ice." Lopez is topographically correct, and historically. And imaginatively, insofar as we were an east-west people. Insofar as we are becoming a north-south people, Americans exist in a region of mind, of spirit, between hot and cold. And we feel ourselves in the middle, an edgy, extreme place to be, as so-called Midwesterners know, especially in summer, especially on those afternoons when satiric Canadian air collides with the flatteries of the Gulf. Then tornadoes tumble cows in the sky, babies rock in the treetops, swimming pools fly and birds are dashed to the ground.

■ ■ ■

My father died of neither hot nor cold. My father was as leathern as a saint. He required no trees. As unrefreshed as a Muslim courtyard. He required no fountain. No music. Whenever he saw a baby he said "poor baby." His questions were the basic questions, as prosaic as footsteps.

What is heaven like?
Will I be young?
Will I be with Mama?
Will I go to sleep? (I don't know, Papa; how can I know?)

Absurdly, I gave answers.

FOR HIM.

Minatitlán, Colima, 1905–San Francisco, California, 2001

- *Chapter Eight* •

GONE WEST

THAT SUMMER I WAS STILL YOUNG ENOUGH TO CALL THE last summer of my youth, I drove cross-country with three college friends. From the freeway on-ramp at Thirtieth and J Streets in Sacramento to the Lincoln Tunnel.

Or bust.

We left California after dinner. Around midnight, we reached Reno where men wearing cowboy hats were pumping gas at the Chevron station. I had never been so far west before, which is to say, so far east.

Native Californians always spoke of the West as though it lay east of here. Any imagination I had of the West (a landscape suggested by studio backlots in Burbank, which was south) lay east. The Sierra Nevada appeared on the horizon, a sheer and dreadful portal from which the Donner Party would never descend. In summer, the range was obscured by Zeusy yellow clouds; sometimes storms of lightning—Olympian ruminations never communicated to the valley floor.

Except in the writings of John Muir. In 1869, Muir spent a summer traversing the Sierra. His more provocative ruminations ran to the California coastline. Muir had arrived in San Francisco by ship and he grasped the implication of the coast. America, he saw, comes to an end here.

I paid the cowboy for the gas. From the moth-intoxicated brightness of the Chevron station, I launched the car once more into the dark. The others were asleep. I listened to Wolfman Jack on a 50,000-watt L.A. radio station. Several hundred miles across the desert, just before dawn, the earth curved. The radio station's grip loosened, shredded into static, released me.

American myth has traditionally been written east to west, describing an elect people's manifest destiny accruing from Constitution Hall to St. Jo' to the Brown Palace Hotel to the Golden Gate. Now a classics professor in Oregon rebuts my assertion that California is not the West. His family moved to Anaheim from Queens. They moved *west*. Simple. The way the East Coast has always imagined its point of view settled the nation.

In Warner Bros.' cartoons the sun went down with a *kerplop* and a hiss into an ocean that had to be the Pacific. Because I assumed I knew where the day ended, the more interesting question was: Where does the West begin?

I recall James Fenimore Cooper's description of a lighted window on the frontier. No place else in American literature does a candle burn so brightly. That small calix of flame was a beacon of the East—all the fame of it. Where the light from the candle was extinguished by darkness, there the West began.

A couple of years ago, at a restaurant in the old train station in Pittsburgh (as coal cars rumbled past our table), my host divulged an unexpected meridian: "Pittsburgh is the gateway to the West." The same in St. Louis; the same in Kansas City. At a Mexican restaurant in Texas: Dallas is where the East begins; Forth Worth is where the West begins.

We did bust.

In Iowa. I can't remember what the matter was—probably the water pump. It was eastern influence that drew us on. Chris's father knew an executive for the Ford Motor Company. Phones rang in Des Moines on a Sunday morning. The Ford Motor dealership summoned their mechanic from his recliner.

At Stanford University, in those last years of the sixties, we referred, not yet with irony, to "Western civ." I remember one professor's observation that, whereas the *Iliad* is tragic (good men die; the mediocre survive), the *Odyssey* is comic (a restoration). Ever after, I would imagine my coming life, in retrospect, as comic.

I was a baby boomer. I believed in movement. That was the theme of California. People were coming to California to begin life anew; I believed in the necessity of abandoning Sacramento, if I were ever to amount to anything. But it was the same impulse. I assumed there would be room enough on the freeway for my ambition.

I was trained east. Louis L'Amour and Zane Grey wrote "westerns." Westerns sold for twenty-five cents to old men with wires running from their ears down to the batteries in their shirt pockets; men who would otherwise spend their evenings staring at the linoleum.

I was trained east, an inveterate reader of "easterns": Wharton, James, Kazin, Baldwin, O'Hara. I noticed the highest easterns—Wharton, James—were written as though they were westerns (the arrival of an innocent). Isabel Archer of Albany, New York, journeys to Europe where she achieves inexperience amidst the etiolated foliage, the thicker light, the thinner blood, the charged conversations.

We crossed the Mississippi around nine o'clock Sunday night. I remember thinking we had left the West behind.

Go East, young woman! I think we are just now beginning to discern an anti-narrative—the American detective story told from west to east, against manifest destiny, against the early Protestant point of view, against the Knickerbocker Club, old Ivy, the assurances of New England divines.

Josiah Royce, Nick Carraway, Damon Runyan, Lynn O'Donnell—for many of us who had grown up west of the Mississippi, New York was finishing school. Eating clubs at Princeton, Eliot House, authority, memory—all the un-American themes. After Lynn died it seemed imperative to get her obituary into the *New York Times*.

I remember thinking nothing could be more glamorous than to be the *New Yorker* correspondent who would hold any hinterland—be it Paris, Rio, or Sacramento—up to the amused monocle of Eustace Tilley. An entire literature of the West was made up of such correspondents: Harte, Muir, Twain. Coldest winter I ever spent was one summer in *Saaan Francisco.* HAW. HAW. HAW.

Oh, god, now bored Athene, heavily rouged, reaches down through cloud cover into history to pluck the scrolling arrow in its flight, to bend it backward; watch the joke.

A florid, balding gymnopede bellows to me from an adjacent StairMaster that he is abandoning California. "Too . . . ," he raises fur-epauleted shoulders to portray constriction. He is moving "out West"—that is the expression he uses—to a house on three acres, thirty minutes from Boise where there are still trees and sky.

To find where the West begins I will need to follow Athene's U-turned arrow straight through nineteenth-century Wall Street, across the Atlantic to Enlightenment Paris, down the bronzed coast of Western civilization to ancient Greece.

The Greeks associated identity with action. The heroic ideal is the active life. I think of Odysseus. Specifically, the last book of the *Odyssey*—Homer unable to finish his tale. Odysseus, father to Telemachus, son to Laertes, finds his way home to resume his rightful role as husband to Myrna Loy. But the ordered world, prepared and preserved by the heroic deed, does not suit. What, after all, does the achievement of stasis mean for the warrior whose very name connotes wandering?

Such is the rate of change in the West, you end up sounding like some hoary Ancient if you recollect the fragrance of almond orchards where the mystic computer chip clicks; if you remember cattle where almond trees bloom. I meet such middle-aged ancients. The man in Albuquerque has seen his hometown completely changed in forty-two years, even the sky. "They" have changed everything. They, presumably, are his own parents.

The limitation of the Greek ideal is apparent the morning after you have found your way home. The curtains are drawn. The room is close. Too many ruffles. You stare at the ceiling. You look at your watch. Now what?

Now shit-souled Athene has to invent Vietnam because Odysseus still has his muscle tone and a ripe old age is part of his contract. He signs on for another pic.

Left behind, Myrna Loy seeks an aperture as her life constricts to ice cubes and Cablevision. She does not for a moment consider California when she decides to retire in the West. She settles in Santa Fe with its ancient, reassuring patina recently applied with little sponges. She wears blue jeans; nods to "Howdy"; she goes to the opera; sometimes to Mass.

The apparent flattery the East Coast pays California is that the future begins here. Hula hoops, beatniks, Proposition 13, LSD, skateboards, silicon chips, Malibu Buddhism. California, the laboratory; New York, the patent office. The price Californians pay for such flattery is that we agree to be seen as people lacking in experience, judgment, and temper. It seems not to have occurred to the East that because the West has a knowledge of the coastline, the Westerner is the elder, the less innocent party in the conversation.

Californians have been trying to tell Eastern America that our nation is, after all, finite. Only within the last few years—a full century after the closing of the frontier—have we gotten a bite on the cliché: *Tonight, Peter Jennings asks: Is the Golden State tarnished?*

A few years ago, after an earthquake in Los Angeles, a tele-vision producer for the Canadian Broadcasting Corporation asked for an interview on the future of California. There had been a race riot in Los Angeles. The Berkeley hills had burned. Floods in the canyons had carried away a Topanga grand-mother. The Canadian producer decided we would have our televised conversation at Venice Beach, the place tourists come on Sundays to experience comic extremity by the sea. I would sit in an Adirondack chair, the blue Pacific over my shoulder.

And, by and by, there I was on Venice Beach, wired for sound and my hair blowing east. I had become a correspon-dent. But this was Tuesday, a gray afternoon, the fog pouring in on a gale. Teenagers wearing Raiders jackets stomped over ca-bles that were lying about, kids so accustomed to TV crews they didn't even pause to gander. An old guy wanted five bucks to stay out of the shot. A trio of German tourists, two men and a woman, and they all looked like Beethoven, stopped at each of the hundred and one T-shirt and counterfeit stands that lined the beach. The Tarot readers set up their card tables and sat with their backs to the gray ocean, limp-haired priestesses of that monotonous turbine. Panning the scene for something golden to shoot, we did eventually find one happy face—at the concrete Muscle Beach exhibition booth, a sunburned old salt with sagging breasts, eager to pose for the camera in his red ny-lon bikini, winking insanely with every revolution and flex.

Athene roars with laughter; switches channels.

An arrow pointing straight up: LINCOLN TUNNEL. A thun-derstorm hid the famous ruminant skyline whose opinions I had memorized through thousands of pages. Following the arrow, we found ourselves immediately in the heart of the city. Theaters were letting out. The Booth, the Plymouth. We turned right. People waited for cabs under an awning at 21. Park Avenue. Thirty blocks of glorious redundancy. When we got to Chris's building, several doormen, uniformed like Soviet generals, advanced to seize our luggage.

In the morning, Chris's mother half turned from her correspondence to ask if I had brought along my dinner jacket. There was to be a party on Thursday at the Met for "Tom" and his new wife. Downstairs, a doorman stood watching the slow progress of traffic along Park Avenue.

Morning, Eddie.

Chris and I found a diner on Lexington Avenue. A Greek waiter threw down two wet plastic menus. I opened mine with the satisfaction of having achieved my American novel. At the top, under *Good Morning*—cock-a-doodle-do and the rising sun—I read: **SACRAMENTO TOMATO JUICE**.

▪   ▪   ▪

Several seasons ago Ralph Lauren produced fashion layouts of high WASP nostalgia that were also confused parables of Original Sin. Bored, beautiful children pose upon the blue lawns of Long Island, together with their scented, shriven parents. All are washed in the Blood of the Lamb. The parents have rewon Eden for the sake of the children. The knowing children, however, have found a disused apple under the hedge and have shared it.

Mr. Lauren's later work attempted a less complicated innocence; he had himself photographed astride a horse. The
mise-en-scène became the American West. According to *W*
magazine, in real life (as we say, allowing for variance), whenever Mr. Lauren wants to escape the rag trade in New York, he
repairs to his Double RL Ranch, a 14,000-acre spread outside
Telluride, Colorado.

On a meadow within that reserve, Mr. Lauren has constructed a Plains Indian teepee, inside which he has placed
club chairs from London and Navajo rugs, electrical outlets,
phones, CDs—"stuff an Indian never dreamed of," one ranch
hand remarks.

I do not intend to mock Mr. Lauren's *Trianon sauvage*. It may
represent an authentic instinct for survival, like the family-
built nuclear shelters of the 1950s. Leaving all that alone, I
should confess I have not made my own peace with wilderness,
never liking to be more than two miles from restaurants and
theaters. From an air-conditioned car, I often regret suburban
sprawl. That is an aesthetic regret. As a Westerner, I must approve the human domination of Nature.

I have been to Telluride only once, for the film festival. Often enough of late I have visited those chic little towns that
nestle in the mountain states of the West. Lynn's wedding in
Idaho, most recently—the guests had flown in from L.A. and
London. On the Saturday morning, nearly everyone rode into
the foothills on horseback.

Whereas I trudged one mile, perhaps two, in the direction of
loneliness. A noise stopped me. A crackle or something; a

pinecone dropping; a blue jay. I think I did discover an anxiety the pioneers could have known in these same woods a century ago. Injuns? Well, but I am an Indian, and my shoes were getting scuffed. Maybe the woods were dangerously settled? Snow White and her Seven Militiamen? And then a prospect far more unsettling: The forest was empty. I turned and quickly walked back to the lodge, where Ella Fitzgerald's voice flitted through speakers in the eaves of the lobby.

Mr. Lauren, quoted in *W,* speaks in oracular puffs from beneath designer blankets: "I'm just borrowing the land." (. . .) "You can never really own it." (. . .) The *W* article notes, however, that the Double RL Ranch is circumscribed by fifteen miles of white fence.

Wisdom and a necessary humility inform the environmental movement, but there is an arrogant self-hatred, too, in the idea that we can create landscapes vacant of human will. In fact, protection is human intrusion. The ultimate domestication of Nature is the ability to say: Rage on here, but not elsewhere!

In nineteenth-century daguerreotypes of the American West, the land is the dropped rind from a transcendently fresh sky. Time is evident; centuries have bleached the landscape. There is no evidence of history, except the presence of the camera. The camera is debris; the pristine image "taken" is contamination. The camera can only look backward; our appraisal of the photograph is pure and naïvely fond. To see the future we must look through Ray-Bans darkly.

Puritan theology predisposed pioneers to receive this land as the happy providence of God. The gift must have inspired exhilaration, for settlers damned the waters, leveled mountains, broke their backs to build our regret.

An acquaintance in his eighties recently had pits of cancer dug out of the side of his nose. My friend lamented his disfiguring fate in the present tense: "I use sunscreen; never go out without a hat." The young doctor's prognosis harkened to a pristine West: "This damage was done a long time ago, when you were a little boy and stayed too long in the sun."

I believe those weathered Westerners who tell me over the roar of their air conditioners that the wilderness is no friend. They seem to have at least as true a knowledge of the West as the Sierra Club church. A friend, an ex–New Yorker, now a Californian, tells me she was saved from a panic attack, driving one night through New Mexico, by a sudden blaze of writing in the sky: **Best Western**.

I was driving myself to the sea on a twisting wilderness road. Each mountain turn revealed new curtailed vistas, kliegs of sunlight, rocks spilled at the side of the road. Then another turn and, in a clearing, a bungalow, a lawn, a coiled hose, a satellite dish. *What an absurdity, thought Goldilocks, to plant Pasadena here.*

Something in the heart of the Westerner must glory in the clamor of hammers, the squealing of saws, the rattle of marbles in aerosol cans. Something in the heart of the Westerner must yearn for lost wilderness, once wilderness has been routed. That in us which is most and least human—I mean the soul—cannot live at ease with oblivious nature. Nor do we live easily with what we have made. We hate both the world without us and the world we create. (Bad suburban architecture hints at good Augustinian theology—we are meant for some other world.) So we mythologize. Ralph Lauren has built roads, sunk ponds, cleared pastures. "My goal is to keep and preserve the West."

Lauren's teepee of "commercially farmed buffalo hides" was painted by a "local mountain man" with figures representing Mr. and Mrs. Lauren and their three children.

Once the shopping center is up and the meadows are paved over and the fries are under the heat lamp, we park in a slot, take our bearings, and proceed to the Cineplex to watch Pocahontas's hair commune with the Great Conditioner. We feel ourselves very sympathetic with the Indian, a sympathy we extend only to the dead Indian. Weeping Conscience has become the patron saint of an environmental movement largely made up of the descendants of pioneers. More curiously, the dead Indian has come to represent pristine Nature in an argument made by some environmentalists against "overpopulation" (the fact that so many live Indians in Latin America are having so many babies and are advancing north).

That part of me I will always name western first thrilled at the West in VistaVision at the Alhambra Theater in Sacramento, in those last years before the Alhambra was torn down for a Safeway. In the KOOL summer dark, I took the cowboy's side. Now the odds have shifted. All over the West, Indians have opened casinos where the white man might test the odds.

Another summer day, late in the 1960s: I was driving a delivery truck for the Holbrecht Light Company to a construction site at the edge of Sacramento. Making a sharp right turn, I saw a gray snake keeling through the mirage of water upon the asphalt. I make no apology for that snake. It is no literary device I conjure to make a theological point. It was really there in the delivery truck's path on that summer afternoon for the same reason that Wyoming sunsets resemble bad paintings.

I hadn't time enough to swerve or to stop. *Bump. Bump.* Front wheels; back wheels. Looking into the rearview mirror, I saw the snake writhing, an intaglio of pain. I drove on.

Eventually, I found the empty new house where I made my delivery. After a few minutes, I returned to my truck, retraced my way out of the maze. Only then did I remember the snake and look for it, where I had run over it.

Several construction workers were standing alongside a sandwich truck, drinking sodas. One man, a dark Mexican, shirtless, had draped the snake I killed over his shoulders—an idea that had not yet occurred to Ralph Lauren who, at that time, was just beginning to be preoccupied with high WASP nostalgia.

▪ ▪ ▪

Here in San Francisco, in summer, sleeping revelers incorporate an aching horn into the narratives of their dreaming. Coast Guard officials tried a few years ago replacing foghorns with more efficient sonar, but the citizenry wouldn't hear of it. After a hundred years, we demanded our accustomed meteorologic lullaby. Foghorns were reinstalled at taxpayers' expense, and worth every penny, for those accustomed to being awakened

know it is the horn that makes fog—whimsically and at concu-
piscent intervals—manufactures fog to puff it under the bridge
or pump it down the hills to swill about the wharves. Bellows
atop poles broadcast the agnostic alarm with a basso blast—
Boris Godunov in H_2O.

*You are alive, you are alone, tomorrow is not yet dry, go
back to sleep.*

Except for the sound of a horn, fog never enters a room. Or
swirls about an opened door, as in B-movies. Even when you
are engulfed by it, fog remains distance—not even as tangible
as regret. There is nothing to be done, nothing to cancel or
celebrate—picnics, plane flights, executions will all take place—
nothing but to note the conditional. The unclear. The tarnished.
You are alive. You wake up staring. Turn away from the parted
curtain. Another foggy day.

▪ ▪ ▪

This summer I am mordant enough to name the last summer
of my youth (it is the afternoon of my fiftieth birthday), I have
come to Point Reyes, a promontory from which one can see
for miles along the coast of California, north and south. The
ocean, seen from this height, is tarpaulin.

Just below the lighthouse, warning signs have been posted by
the National Park Service. There are photographs of nineteenth-
century shipwrecks. Cautions to swimmers. Illustrations of the
physics of undertow. Charts of species of shark. *Beware, beware . . .*

Whales pass by here.

I descend to the water's edge. Appropriate for a middle-aged man to turn up his collar, roll his cuffs, and play at the edge. The ocean is young—unraveling and then snatching back its grays and pinks, celadons, and the occasional bonny blue. The relentless flirtation of it loses charm.

Adam and Eve were driven by the Angel of the Fiery Sword to a land east of Eden, there to assume the burden of time, which is work and death. All photosynthetic beings on earth live in thrall to the movement of the sun, from east to west. Most babies are born in the early morning; most old people die at sunset, at least in novels of large theme. We know our chariot sun is only one of many such hissing baubles juggled about, according to immutable laws.

Fuck immutable laws. Fuck mutability, for that matter. I just had my face peeled. I go to the gym daily. I run. I swallow fistfuls of vitamins. I resort to scruffing lotions and toners. Anywhere else in the world I could pass for what-would-you-say? In California, I look fifty.

Besides. The older I become, the further I feel myself from death. It is the young who are dying. A few days before her death, Lynn and I came to this beach. She wore a red baseball cap over her bald head. Lynn regretted the impression our bodies left in the tall grass over there. She took off her sunglasses to face the brightening scrim with burnt-out eyes. I wondered, at the time, if she was forcing herself to remember this place for eternity or if she was consigning herself to Nature (the motion of the sea intent upon erasure).

I remain unreconciled to the logic of an alleged Nature. I am unnatural. As a boy, I read Richard Henry Dana's *Two Years Before the Mast*. What I remember is the furious storm as the ship tossed about the Horn, all Nature pitched against us. My Dana was not the Dana whom D. H. Lawrence mocked for returning to Boston, to Harvard, to a clerk's position, a clerk's fizzing kettle. My Dana was a white-throated, red-lipped romantic who sailed away.

Odd the convergence of loss and rescue at one place. A few years before, Lynn met a malign shade here. She had been picnicking with a friend from New York when the shadow of a rifle trespassed upon their blanket. *Pick up your things!* In the guise of gathering, Lynn slammed a purple-spilling bottle against the shadow's skull, then kicked its softer groin. The two women ran through the tall grass, across the parking lot, to safety.

Around the rock where I am sitting now, seabirds gather to rotate their silly heads; zoom unblinking lenses toward my fists, patient for the manna I might be concealing there. It is the last day of July, the feast of St. Ignatius. The wind is picking up and the waves come pounding in from the gray towers of Asia.

This morning I had been studying an illustration on perspective in the encyclopedia because I was interested to understand the vanishing point. Might not the vanishing point allow for another, an inverted vision, an opposite vertical angle? If lines of perspective cross at one point, might they not continue after that point to open up again? This is the same day I read in the paper that the universe is flat; that the universe is expanding outward, rather than gathering to a foamy flush as those galactic photographs suggest. I begin to imagine pagodas and lanterns, gardens of spice, that lie beyond this scrim.

Imagine how California must have appeared to those first Europeans—the Spaniards, the English, the Russians—who saw the writing of the continent in reverse, from the perspective of Asia, adjusting their view of the coast through a glass, silent and as predatory as these birds.

The little person in the encyclopedia illustration of perspective is me. A little man wearing a suit. He is fifty. Little dotted lines travel from his eyes out to the horizon (which we shall call the Pacific) to stop at the vanishing point. The dotted lines are tears. That much we know. But where is Lynn? That is the question confounding all perspective.

Lynn again: *"What if . . . ?"* As we toured an exhibition of Japanese armor, Lynn marked the similarity of Samurai headdresses to American Indian war bonnets, buffalo heads, horns, plumage. *"What if the Americas had been discovered by Japan, rather than Spain?"*

What if? What if you are not a clump of sea grass, my darling? What if your pleased soul rides a lantern-rigged gondola through the Catholic arrondissement?

By the time he returned to the East Coast, Richard Henry Dana was about the same age I was when I moved to Los Angeles. I was determined to throw off all clerkishness. Only to become a writer. Twenty-five years ago in L.A., one sensed anxiety over some coming "change" of history, having to do with finitude and recurrence.

Rereading Dana, I am struck by the obvious. Dana saw California as an extension of Latin America. Santa Barbara, Monterey, San Francisco—these were Mexican ports of call. Dana would not be surprised, I think, to find Los Angeles today a Third World capital teeming with Aztec and Maya. He would not be surprised to see that California has become what it already was in the 1830s.

From its American occupation, Los Angeles took its reflection from the sea, rather than the desert. Imagined itself a Riviera. Knowledge of the desert would have been akin to a confession of Original Sin—land connection to Mexico was a connection to a culture of death. Los Angeles was preoccupied with juvenescence.

More than aridity, America fears fecundity. Perhaps as early as the 1950s' film *Invasion of the Body Snatchers,* nightmare images of pregnant pods and displacing aliens converge. Fecundity is death. (To manufacture life is to proliferate death.) Who's going to pay for fecundity? The question reminds us of scarcity, for we live at the edge of the sea. What is scarce is water. Metaphors Californians summon today to describe the fear of the South are, appropriately, fluid. Waves of people coming. Tides of immigrants. Floods of illegals. Sand, the primordial image of barrenness, uncivilization, becomes an image of unchecked fertility.

The reflection of the sea has its perils, too. One Sunday in December 1941, Hawaii became the point on the map Americans would remember as our vulnerability to Asia. After the war, Hawaii began our boast: *The Pacific is ours.*

Nineteenth-century California resisted the Asian approach. Though coolie labor built much of the American West, Chinese laborers were persecuted by California for coming at the continent from the fishy side. Celestials, we called them, had a devilish language of crossed sticks and broken banjo strings. The custody they exercised over their eyes inferred they had discovered evil here but they were keeping the knowledge to themselves. Inscrutable, we said at the time.

Now Californians complain that Asians are taking all the desks at the University of California.

Coming upon the continent from the Atlantic, English Puritans imagined the land as prehistoric; themselves cast onto Eden. The Indian they named Savage, rather than Innocent, keeping innocence for themselves. The Atlantic myth of Genesis worked so powerfully on the first non-native imaginations that future generations of Americans retained the assumption of innocence—a remarkably resilient psychic cherry. Every generation of Americans since has had to reenact the loss of our innocence. Smog over L.A. was the loss of our innocence. Vietnam was the loss of our innocence. Gettysburg was the loss of our innocence. Ingrid Bergman's baby was the loss of our innocence. Oklahoma City was the loss of our innocence. The World Trade Center was the loss of our innocence. Other nations are cynical. America has preferred the child's game of "discovering" evil—Europe's or Asia's, her grandfather's, even her own.

The east-west dialectic in American history reasserted man's license to dominate Nature—the right endeavor of innocence.

Railroad tracks binding the continent are vestigial stitches of the smoke-belching Judeo-Christian engine, Primacy o' Man. Having achieved the Pacific Coast, settlers turned to regret the loss of Nature. That is where the West begins.

Twice a year, along this coast, crowds gather to watch the epic migration of whales, north to south, south to north. The route of the whale holds great allure for postmodern Californians, because it is prehistoric, therefore anti-historical (as we will ourselves to be), free of all we disapprove in human history. The Pacific totem pole might be an emblem for a New Age, marking the primacy of Nature over man—a new animistic north-south dialectic that follows a biological, solstitial, rather than a historical, imperative.

The old east-west dialectic in America moved between city and country, the settled and the unsettled. The plaid-suited city slicker disembarked at the western terminus of the nineteenth century to find himself an innocent amidst the etiolated foliage, the overwhelming light, the thicker blood, the conversations in Spanish. Today's children, children of the suburbs, hitch between tundra and desert, Alaska and Baja, cold and hot—versions of extremity beyond which unpolluted Nature lies or oblivion or God.

The sole religious orthodoxy permitted in our public schools is the separation of paper from plastic. Not so many miles from this beach, great-grandchildren of westering pioneers chain themselves to redwoods, martyrs of the new animism.

There is a stand of eucalyptus in Pacific Grove, seventy miles, as the crow flies, from where I stand. Californians have for years gathered there to experience themselves as northerly, as spiritually related to Nature. It is a skimpy, tawdry sort of Nature, in fact—a city block in length, in depth—surrounded by motels. This grove is the meetinghouse, nay, nothing so plain; this grove is the cathedral of the Monarch butterfly. Every autumn, caravans of ragged wings propel themselves hence according to some fairy compulsion. It is a mystic site. We stand with our mouths agape; we look up, up, up—*Look! I see them!*—circling clouds of stained-glass wings descending in a gyre. Despite the surroundings, the beauty of them is so surprising, so silent, so holy as to be wounding to the soul, for they resemble what clouds of angels in baroque paintings resemble, what toccata and fugue resemble, or what galactic kaleidoscope resembles.

I assume you know more about butterflies than I do. I experience awe, not expecting to, but do I misunderstand the thrall of instinct displayed to me? The solemnity is one of death, is it not, as much as of beauty? The spectator infers from this rite that the individual life does not matter. The pattern matters. Generation matters.

There are things one must do. There are things one should do. Moral imperatives propel my soul's journey. One's human instinct is to murmur superstitiously, to enumerate the things one must do before Nature pulls one under. One is drawn nevertheless into this beguiling gyre. For these angels describe existence softly, silently as petals fall. We cannot hear the engine that has shredded them. We see only flecks of amber, drift of blossoms. These angels are several generations removed from ancestors who departed this grove last year; several generations removed from ancestors who will return next fall. They alight to hang like sere leaves upon the branches. As the sun turns its face from them, they quieten; some will die, fall, blow away, to catch with scraps of paper, gum wrappers, and twists of cellophane in the crevices of logs. But others will gather strength, others will hoist sail to rise like windmills on torrents of air, to worship, I suppose; to submit once more to the same cruel engine, the same piercing joy that grinds the sea.

The liturgy of the Roman Mass still gathers a people *from age to age, so that from east to west a perfect offering may be made.* But from Asia come ancient, bland choreographies, ceremonies not based upon progress or time or moral perfection, but upon the experience of the moment, the balance of chi, an invisible Art Nouveau.

Sometimes my morning walk will take me through Mountain Lake Park in San Francisco. The lake is natural, prehistoric; now endangered. California Indians once lived thereabouts. It was there the Spanish explorer de Anza set up camp in 1776, having climbed on foot from Sonora, Mexico. It is there, early in the morning, I find conventuals of the moment, Chinese widows and widowers in pastel sweat suits interacting with the vacant air; they are rehearsing the rituals of tai chi, their faces lifted toward the brightening sky. I envy them this dumb articulation. It is not prayer, is it? It is balance. But it is complete. The gestures are complete. Slowly, patiently revolving in the moment, as purposeful, as purposeless as butterflies.

Tai chi, yoga, Zen, whooshes of air, some of them; some of them stillnesses—each seeks the moment, the reverberating moment. And feng shui—an intuition for freeing the paths of energy throughout the physical world. I believe this western beach, where I stand, is a vast portal for some such impulse flowing into America, the gate through which the wind-colored dragon flies. The dragon clutches in its claws one empty egg, translucent, fragile, or perhaps it is a dense, dead pearl.

I can see him now, yes, I can see him, a proper Chinatown dragon with silver pompons nodding so gaily upon his spine, his beard of silver fringe, his four, six, eight, hundreds, thousands of athletic, hairless legs, rosy at the calf—*crash-gong-crash-gong*—mincing up to where I stand. He tosses his leonine head. He regards me silently. I tie a garland of green leaves and red firecrackers onto a bamboo pole to feed the droll monster. I raise the pole sky-high. The silver dragon rolls his ping-pongy eyes and rocks from side to side and then begins to writhe upward into the sky, one segment standing upon the shoulders of the next; his mouth clacking open and shut with puppet relish.

East meets East upon this shore. The dragon will discover his tail at last. And within bright paradox another lies: The numerical rise of the Hispanic in America today is paralleled by the numerical rise of the Asian. The Asian moves east into the American West to meet the Hispanic immigrant who moves north to reach the American West. The Hispanic brings the idea of a continuous past into a country that preferred to think of time as forward thrust. The Asian brings the idea of moment, of the present, into an America that was preoccupied by the westward movement into the future. America is fated to recognize itself as intersection—no, nothing so plain as intersection—as coil, pretzel, Gordian knot with a wagging tail.

The dragon, delighted with his savory, articulates downward from on-high—his shoulders jump down from his back, his back from his hind, a plume of fog issues from his throat like a long dun scarf. Once more the dragon rolls his head, his mane a crashing wave. He takes the sleeve of my coat into his silken jaw to lead me to a copse of sand a few years distant.

Where we sit, dear Lynn, huddled in a present tense, hidden by the tall grass, you in your baseball cap, dark glasses. Me a dry-eyed Indian Catholic praying for the sun to stop its course.

Your ashes scattered over a meadow in Idaho where only the northern winds can find them.

I tell you heaven may be architecturally more substantial than you imagine. You tell me you have always loved this beach because it was here, as a little girl, you first saw an order of angels, the great whales, passing, substantially, between death and birth.

Come now. Whichever the case. See how the metaphor of the West dissolves into foam at our feet.

■ *Chapter Nine* ■

PETER'S AVOCADO

*Can't you see that nothing that goes into someone from out-
side can make that person unclean, because it goes not into
the heart but into the stomach and passes into the sewer?*

—Mark 7:14

I DON'T KNOW IF YOU HAVE EVER LUNCHED WITH A VEGETARIAN.
Probably you have. If you live in San Francisco you have. Then
you've seen Dominic, his hand raised, fingers slightly crook'd
to summon a waitress: *Ma'am?* (Pointing to the menu.) *Is this
dish made with meat stock?* The waitress (a Chinese restaurant) takes a moment to divine the desired answer. No. (When
in doubt.) So imperial, so sliding scale, so uncomprehending is
her no, so wise is her no, finally, so Greek, so Arab, so Catholic,
so Brown is her no, Dominic cannot be reassured. Dominic's
vegetarianism has to do with upholding the sacredness of life.
He needs a puritan answer.

Whereas Peter. Peter is the son of my friend Franz. Peter is
as easy in the brown world of maybe as he is in his own white
skin. He is wandering through India as I write this. Peter is
handsome, gentle, Hindu-intoxicated, slightly blue; his skin is

slightly blue. Peter's veganism has to do with the sacredness of his own body; with the purity of his lungs and his bowels and his liver and his breath. Peter's vigilance is maniacal: *Do you place meat and vegetables on the same grill?*

Franz, Peter's father, with whom I am having lunch at yet another Chinese restaurant (this one called the Mayflower), tells me a story. I have just told Franz my book is about brown—not skin, but brown as impurity—and Franz says, "I have been thinking about purity."

A few months before, before Peter left for India, before I write this, Franz was leaving his house to keep some appointment when Peter called out to him: "Dad, I need you to pick up an avocado on your way home." (Peter, as you may imagine, cooks for himself when he visits home.) The door reopens: "Dad, it has to be an *organic* avocado."

On his way home, Franz stops at Safeway. He notices the small display of organic avocados. He notices organic avocados are expensive but look paltry somehow. He notices the larger display of chemical avocados, much cheaper. He is tempted. At Safeway, of all places, Franz has come upon the fruit of the Tree of the Knowledge of Good and Evil; has even stumbled upon the first theological debate: Will Peter know the difference? Which leads inevitably to the second theological debate: Can what Peter doesn't know defile him?

It is not that Franz would ever harm Peter. What father would harm a son? (Christ asks.) (As the congregation is inevitably reminded of Abraham and Isaac.) Still, Franz is nothing if not deliberate.

▪ ▪ ▪

When the white, wooden Baptist church, a black church, gets torched on a dark night, or when, in the morning light, the synagogue in Illinois is discovered to have been spray-painted with crooked black lines, then holy men gather in front of television cameras to declare themselves united against "hate crimes." They link arms. How they are composed to oppose hate! What the holy men do not say, however, is that love has always been a bigger problem for churches.

As for historians. Say what you will about hate, hate is not ambiguous. Historians with bow ties who win bronze medallions for their labors have long told the story of America as stories of hate—vignettes with clean endings, sharp corners, palls of certainty stretched over the toes and noses of soldiers. History has a beginning, a middle, an outcome. Many appendices, many misgivings, many motives have been summarized. For example, about the woodshed at Monticello, the historians with bow ties were unable to tell us or were disinclined. About the honeyed light through slats in the wall; about motes of dust in the air or the smell of excrement, the buzzing flies. We now are able to scope DNA, and we do so as if we are looking backward through a telescope. We find the course of American history muddies considerably by that reading. And this is clarifying.

American history books I read as a boy were all about winning and losing, contest, vanquishment. One side won; the other side lost; women clutched babes; minstrels composed lays. Children closed their eyes to memorize dates and heard only the buzzing of flies. But what was lost? What won? An acre? A precept? An SAT score? Only the score is remembered. Not the circlet of hair in the oval locket. Not the early frost in the letter, not the breakfast chucked up, not the barometric pressure; the droplet of sweat upon the rib cage; the concussion of the earth, the translucent centipede scrambling for cover. And so it went. So it goes. The progress of a nation, as of a life, is a litany of conflict, score, segment. From conclusion to inception. Conclusion, it is arranged, will stand as the inception of the next segment. It is like balancing books at a business college. And all history books are balanced, as balanced as books in a business college. We can see that one action follows from another in a certain way. The number of dead men who do not prevail against an idea. One political party defeats another political party. One idea in America ascends, another falls. Strikers are mown down by policemen. The tycoon in a dinner jacket leaps to his death or simply eats dinner.

▪ ▪ ▪

The stories in the history book that interested me were stories that seemed to lead off the page: A South Carolina farmer married one of his slaves. The farmer died. The ex-slave inherited her husband's chairs, horses, rugs, slaves. And *then* what happened? Did it, in fact, happen?

Or, at the mordant conclusion of a frontier battle, after all the bodies have been counted and pockets gone through, a single observer—and we wonder what happened to him—describes a mountain man leaving the scene, entering the forest with an Indian woman.

I want to speak of such unpursued scenes and lives as constituting brown history. Brown, not in the sense of pigment, necessarily, but brown because mixed, confused, lumped, impure, unpasteurized, as motives are mixed, and the fluids of generation are mixed and emotions are unclear, and the tally of human progress and failure in every generation is mixed, and unaccounted for, missing in plain sight.

Missing, I suppose, because of the orderly sensibilities of recorders, and then of their readers. We cannot record time. Time is capacious, a rose. Such is what Virginia Woolf intuited. Such is what Marcel Proust intuited. These heroes of the imagination objected to history because the center of it was missing. But they, too, died.

The woman who owned the market around the corner never smiled. I noticed her golden wedding ring. I used to imagine the chime of that ring against a porcelain bowl. But what of that? The market closed. Probably because she never smiled.

That slain boy—the one with the red hair, and of what sort of red?—lies facedown upon a field. A cloud has passed through him, a cloud as soft and as warm as a coverlet has passed through him, has left a blue stain upon his body as it passed. His life is over now, his watch stopped, his fear is pitched away from him like a handful of pitched gravel; all emotion is fled, as if emotions were birds flown from a tree at which gravel has been pitched. Perhaps emotion has flown to the treetops. Perhaps it has flown to the stars. The slain boy is utterly irrelevant to our history.

The history of the day belongs to the redcoated captain

there, florid, morose, in his tent; in truth, it belongs more to his charts and his lamp, than to the powder horn or the sword (though he read the Greeks as a lad). A decrepit sword (his) rests now in a glass case in a museum in Boston with a card of explanation, a legend which has gone unread for many years. The last person to read the card was a girl with brown hair who had run away from home (pregnant) and who tore her last stick of gum in half to save the half for later, and who entered the museum to use the lavatory and she read the legend of the sword and a few others, so as not to appear to have come in just to use the rest room. She left again, walked out into the painful noon and traffic of that lost day, walked up the street two blocks, turned a corner and disappeared.

And what of her observer? What of him?

What of the card? The card was originally, in measurement, 2½ by 3 inches; standard card; manufactured by the American Paper Company in 1908. The card was hand-lettered by Mrs. M_____ C_____ who had a contract with the museum for piecework: "script that shall be legible from a distance of approximately one yard." For many years she gave satisfaction, for many years—this was the latter part of her life—she worked in the best light (a table near a window in the back room), while her husband coughed up his life, half hours, hours, to spit them into rags in the front bedroom—"spittle rags"—and these lay all about the floor and were tucked under his pillow, while Mrs. M_____ C_____ copied legends such as that descriptive of General Whitmarsh's sword, its maker, dimensions, date, inscription, metal. It is not known whether the gray blade ever smote flesh. Mrs. M_____ C_____'s card was replaced by a typewritten card in 1934. That card was retyped in 1954, again in 1960 on an electric.

▪ ▪ ▪

I am the observer.

Every American comes upon the "I," awakens to it. The prow of the ship. The top of the tree. The hilt of the sword. The animate eye. The quick. The reader of the card pertaining to the sword. Very interesting, but now I need to go to the bathroom. The American I. As in, *I believe, I take Jesus Christ as my personal savior. I am sorry for the earthquake victims. I will have tuna on rye. I love you.* The I does not impose solitude, though it is lonely; the I is alive. The I may be an instrument of connection, but even as such it is an assertion of will. *I have my rights.*

As so often happens in America, the I attached to me at school:

You!

Who? I was no longer my brother's brother, my sister's brother, my mother's son, my father's son, my backyard's potentate. I was alone. I . . . I had to go to the bathroom, what should I do?

Go to college, become a man different from your father. It's up to you. Don't go to college, become a man different from your father.

The American I is as old as the Boston Tea Party, as old as the document of Constitution: "We the People . . ."

We? But I am a royalist. As the son of immigrants, I do not

remember America seeming like a choice, though Americans were always and everywhere talking about choices.

They talked about black beans or refried. Presbyterian or Methodist. Ford or Chevrolet. Cinema One or Cinema Two. Gay or straight. CBS or NBC. Paper or plastic. Diet or regular. Regular or decaf. Plain or buttered. White or whole wheat or sourdough or English muffin. Every lighted window, every court, every slug of type, every knuckle of America strained to accomplish my assertion: I am innocent.

I may be unwise, I may be mistaken, I may be guilty. But the essence of the American I is that I am irreducible.

I can be punished for my crime, in other words. Isn't that odd? My body can bear the weight of punishment for a crime weighed in the apprehension of others who did not see, who do not know what I know.

Americans are so individualistic, they do not realize their individualism is a communally derived value. The American I is deconstructed for me by Paolo, an architect who was raised in Bologna: "You Americans are not truly individualistic, you merely are lonely. In order to be individualistic, one must have a strong sense of oneself within a group." (The "we" is a precondition for saying "I.") Americans spend all their lives looking for a community: a chatroom, a church, a support group, a fetish magazine, a book club, a class-action suit.

But illusions become real when we think they are real and act accordingly. Because Americans thought themselves free of plural pronouns, they began to act as free agents, thus to recreate history. Individuals drifted away from tribe or color or 'hood or hometown or card of explanation, where everyone knew who they were. *That's Victoria and Leo's son, isn't it?* Americans thus extended the American community by acting so individualistically, so anonymously.

▪ ▪ ▪

As traitors do. To my unformed eye, the woman sitting on my aunt's sofa looked just like the Clairol Lady of the magazine advertisements of the time. The Clairol Lady was married to the Hindu. That much I got. The Hindu was my Indian uncle's nephew on his dark-scented side, snuff-after-dinner side.

As we came home from that long, heated Christmas dinner—the enforced good behavior seemed an extenuation of the forms of the High Mass the evening previous—my mother grew impatient with my childish pesterings concerning the blond woman who perched so demurely upon my aunt's sofa. The woman's first name was a biblical name. Her last name was his, an Indian name. *But where did she come from?* My finger traced circles within my warm breath on the dark car window. My brother and sisters were asleep. *What is it you want to know, Richard? They met in college.* But that wasn't what I wanted to know.

I had impure thoughts.

I never questioned how we were made. God made us. Or how we were related to India. We were Mexican. They were Indian. Somehow we were all brown. *That thou shouldst descend to mortal clay.* Mortal clay. Ashes to ashes. I was an altar boy. But I wouldn't believe such a blond woman was natural to us.

I had heard the term "ash blond." Perhaps she was an ash blond. She was unnatural is what I meant. Unnatural to us. She was the opposite of divorce, but just as strange. She was the opposite of Adam. She was Eve, coming out of nowhere.

Bless me, Father, for I have sinned. And so I believed, that I had sinned, whenever I confessed to the unseeing voice of Father Edmund O'Neill in the dark confessional box. This was the opposite of punishment.

Pure thoughts are few and far between. Impurities are motives, weights, considerations, temptations that digress from God. I think I'll have hotcakes for breakfast, for example, during the Elevation of the Host. Or, I threw a rock at Billy Walker because I loved him.

Well, who attended the ash-blond wedding? Was it accomplished with saffron robes? With incense? Did they make the blond woman dance some hootchie-kootch dance in a red veil, a diamond stuck in her navel as in a Betty Grable movie?

A young woman from San Jose who writes to me, tells me, by way of introduction, that she is the daughter of a "New York Jew" and an "Iranian Muslim."

That is what I want to know. That is what I want to hear about—children who are unnatural to any parish because they belong to no precedent. Brown children are as old as America—oh, much older—to be the daughter of a father is already to be brown. To be the rib-wife of Adam was already to be brown; to be Adam summoned from dust as the magpies watched and nudged one another. But public admissions of racial impurity are fresh and wonderful to me.

The reason I remain interested in brown history today is because, as a boy, I was embarrassed by my sexual imagination. I was looking for the world entire. I suspected dimensions I could not find—by find I mean read about, I suppose. I never expected to form a "we" beyond my family. When would the impulse come, as it came to the birds, as it came to the bride? That was why the presence of the blond woman disturbed me so. She was proof of some power in the world I could not admit I felt.

Mixed soul, I suspect, may become, in this twenty-first century, what "mixed blood" was for the eighteenth century. A scandal against straight lines and deciduous family trees. Against patriarchs who do not sufficiently recall that Christ formed an alliance of the moment with the Samaritan woman—some spark of wit, perhaps; some amused recognition or willingness that intrigues us still. Perhaps a smile. Already, the assembly of holy men, the rabbis and priests and mullahs agree they do not like it. The brown theology of syncretism abroad in the land—cross-dressed Christmas dinners—the lotus and the holly. That apostasy should form flesh they do not like. My church's definition of "mixed marriage," for example, had nothing to do with blood, I knew that, but with the irreconcilability of questions and answers.

Love conquers all. As does Saturday night at the Rose and Crown. As does the rain that falls on the just and unjust? Is the love of God brown, really, like the love of a man for a woman? Or are you just saying that? That's what I want to know. By brown I mean biological, not some drapery or mist, but spirit stuck in flesh, pitiful, like those mastodons stuck in the La

Brea tar pits, bleating for mamas who died millions of years ago. The love of God beating a path through birth canals in order to call us mama. Is it real?

Painters sometimes refer to brown as a "dead color"—not as in Aramaic, or the bosom of Abraham, but in quietude, slowness to delight, misgiving.

I recently asked a painter which were the brownest paintings he could think of.

He said cubists found their preoccupation with form disallowed a bright palette; nothing more than burlapy brown. The capture of form rather than the capture of light. Form, space, but not progression. There is no time in cubism. All is present tense. The Nude cannot descend the staircase. Though she has reached the bottom, she has not yet left the top.

A texture favored by cubists, an illusion favored by cubists, was the plane of wood. A plane of wood favored by cubists was the table. The table favored by cubists was the table upon which objects had been arranged. Ladies and gentlemen, the table made of wood: *Part the curtain. Stand there. Or over there. Or here. Crawl underneath. Stand here, directly above, careful of the light.* The table, the book, the matchbox, the chessboard, the cigar, the coffee, the *Figaro.* The rock I threw at Billy Walker. All present at once as several points of view. The illustration of a faculty humans intuit, though we do not possess it. A faculty Virginia Woolf intuited. A faculty we ascribe to ghosts or angels. Or cubists.

Cubism, as ghosts might see us: manifest, but without motive; moving through the form of a room, but without motive.

Incapable of recalling a motive for what we are engaged in—
passion, chess, music, absence, descending a staircase—a series of stop-frames fanning out from a pin in the middle, which
is the moment. The moment for which Emily in *Our Town*
pleads: *Do any human beings ever realize life while they live
it?—every, every minute?*

We cannot. We must be mistaken to live. We do notice,
however, how oddly we are constructed, how oddly we are
evolved. Hands. Lips. Birth canals. As are our implements.
Things we pick up and put down. Gloves. Forceps. The way we
must hold the guitar constructs the guitar. It stands to reason.
We have only two hands. The guitar constructs music. Music
constructs silence. (An Icelandic composer interviewed on the
radio said silence constructs music.) Silence constructs hope
or fear. Of ghosts or angels. Cubism is not for angels. For angels, as for Virginia Woolf, motive alone is manifest.

The reason I threw a rock at Billy Walker's stupid face was I
had a crush on him.

*Bless me, Father, for I have sinned. It has been thirty years
since my last confession. I threw a rock at Billy Walker's beautiful face.*

How many times? At what velocity?

The priest does not ask if I intended to mar the face. One of
the things I love about the church is that motive is assumed:
Because I am human. What alone interests the confessor is
the form of humanity I wish to confess. Confession is constructed as we are constructed. The confessional box prefig-
ures the American I.

I am the sinner, irreducible. My soul is irreducible. Not my red hand.

I looked for the impure in everything. I truly looked for a mixture of motive. The stories in the history book that interested me were stories that seemed to lead off the page.

I lived my life in fragments. For I knew nothing was so dangerous in the world as love, my kind of love. By love, I mean my attempt to join the world. My cubist life: My advantage (my sympathy toward brown and the bifocal plane) was due to the fact that from an early age I needed to learn caution, to avert my eyes, to guard my speech, to separate myself from myself from myself. Or to reconstruct myself in some eccentric way— my pipe protruding from my ear, my ear where my nose should be—attempting to compose myself in a chair that slants like a dump shovel. My eyes looking one way, my soul another. My motive could not be integrated with my body, with act or response or, indeed, approval.

And the crucifix, too, superimposed upon my every thought, was a kind of cubism, a private perspective, a quartered plane, a window from which I observed, unobserved, and apparently without motive.

I looked to art to reconcile me to life. But nothing in art is remotely like life. The cross is closer to life than art is.

A man of my acquaintance, now in his seventies, tells me he needed, as a boy, to go to his small town's library in summer, surreptitiously to slide his hand into the liverish side of Noah Webster, to divine what he knew all along he was. This, after he bent over his prep school roommate one night to kiss that sleeping boy. He hadn't meant to. The boy woke up! *What's wrong? Frankie, what's wrong?* Nothing's wrong. Go back to sleep.

The way we are constructed constructs the violin. The violin constructs music. But what of the dulcimer? What of the harp? What of the device that held Bob Dylan's harmonica? What of the French horn? What of the French kiss?

I assure you, music comes first. Or accident. Bones. Spoons. Rubber bands. Boredom creates music. We adapt the physical world to our innate liking—but what is innate? Whatever is music. Love comes first. The first principle comes first. God's love comes first and is not changed, cannot be diminished or turned away by the instrument. Though the symphony, of course, is an invention, a dream of resolution worked out by someone sitting alone.

The way we are constructed constructs love? Limits love? (We die.) The making of love? No. That is a heresy. God so loved the world that the Word became incarnate, condescended to mortal clay. God became brown. True God and true man.

Where there's a will there's a way. Sodomy is among the brownest of thoughts. Even practitioners find it a disagreeable subject. Theological condemnations of sodomy have scrolled into a pillar of negation rising from a small, hometown passage in Genesis wherein some redneck rowdies of Sodom—heterosexuals all, I'd be willing to bet—make obscene remarks about a couple of hunky angels they see passing through town. *Nice suit.*

In an earlier America, some churches, forgetting themselves, pronounced black-and-white love sinful. Churchmen
surfed the Scriptures for any phrase that might pose as an in-
junction against miscegenation. Most churches still unite in
the opinion that homosexuality is a grave moral offense and a
vanity. A priest visiting my parish preached a sermon wherein
he referred to homosexuality as a "lifestyle." By which he
meant a choice. So, too, my beloved Father O'Neill (to whom
I confessed as a child) said to my sister, a few months before
he died, that he disapproved of "Richard's lifestyle."

Homosexuality requires cubism to illustrate itself, perhaps.
But homosexuality is not a lifestyle. Homosexuality is an
emotion—a physiological departure from homeostasis, which
roughly translates as:

> *Shall I compare thee to a summer's day?*
> *Thou art more lovely and more temperate.*

Do not say "I love him" before a convention of Anglican educators at the Fairmont Hotel in San Francisco, though, as I did
(when they thought they had engaged me to speak about "diversity"). Not a few Anglican educators will jump up, as they
did; disinclined to consider my particular diversity. Accept the
invitation to the small Baptist college or the yeshiva or the
Jesuit university, talk about separate races and distinct ethnic-
ities and the divisions in American social life, talk about literature, talk about God. (But do not speak about love.)

I passed many adolescent hours at the Clunie Public Library
in Sacramento, looking—I couldn't have said what I was look-

ing for—I was looking for a brown history of America, I was looking for the precedent that made me possible. I became an amateur student of photographs, of crowds, of the swarming of history, people converging upon the moment. I became a connoisseur of American parades and train stations, drugstores, Armistice Days, state funerals, Fourths of July. Any evidence of exception. What is that lone black man doing in the Irish saloon in New York? I noted black faces at FDR's funeral. I remember an earlier photograph from a book on California—Los Angeles in the 1920s—what looks like a Filipino or Mexican family is standing on the front steps of a small wooden church, within a congregation of African-American women and children. However hard I peered into that long-forgotten day there was no answer. What are they doing there?

Or Francis Parkman's *Oregon Trail*. In 1846, young Parkman left behind the known world to survey the Far West. On his way out, he would meet Mormons, mountain men, Indians. But it was in St. Louis—the first portal of the narrative—that my cubist eye lingered. *What is it you want to know, Richard?* Parkman boards a boat on the sluggish Missouri along with representatives from four corners of history:

> *In her cabin were Santa Fé traders, gamblers, speculators, and adventurers of various descriptions, and her steerage was crowded with Oregon emigrants, "mountain men," Negroes, and a party of Kanzas Indians, who had been on a visit to St. Louis.*

Were such encounters so mundane in this fresh landscape as to require no explanation? What were their smells and seat-ing arrangements; what were the mutterings of uncommon voices? Several races and continents converging in the suspicious glance of eyes. Did I read such proximity as erotic? Indeed, I did. I had no other way to read. I was looking for physical inclusion in the world. I was amassing an encyclopedia of exceptionalism for my own use. What did Negroes infer from the whiny, fiddlelike intonations of mountain men? What, in God's name, had the Kanzas Indians been doing in St. Louis? Were some naked? Were all armed? Blanketed? Beaded? Braided? Painted? Tattooed? Were the smells sordid? Tallow-lit? Shit-smeared? Tobacco-stained? Did all drink from one barrel? Was there danger in every glance? Every nonchalance? As upon the 38 Geary bus in San Francisco?

Parkman does not say.

▪ ▪ ▪

Sitting beside me on the 38 Geary bus, a young man, likely seventeen, stares straight ahead, his eyes apparently concentrating upon what he is listening to, as *tssch, tssch*—the drum and the cymbal—bleed from the earphones of his Sony Walkman. I imagine the young man's privacy as a sunless cave of heavy metal. The expression on his face might pass for gladness.

The 38 Geary Municipal bus line in San Francisco (excluding buses designated "Express") carries roughly 47,000 passengers on an average weekday. The bus runs from the old Transbay Terminal downtown, past Union Square, the Tenderloin, Japan Town, the Western Addition, the Inner Richmond, the Outer Richmond, and on out to sea. Because it is a crosstown line, one commonly overhears Vietnamese, Chinese, Spanish, Tagalog, Japanese, Russian, English. The route from Mission Street to Ocean Beach, moreover, is traveled by many Homeless (an imprecise appellation); downtown for mendicancy; the beach for anonymity. The 38 is not a Missouri riverboat, but is descriptive of diversity as I know it.

Two decades ago, I first noticed Sony Walkmans wrapped around American heads. Surely the Japanese had misconstrued the American market? Tokyo is a city that expresses a peculiarly native talent for the small space—a Japanese discretion for living upon an island and within the confines of a congested city with walls sometimes still constructed of paper. Whereas the hoisted boom box—demanding, thumping, parting the crowd, proclaiming one's existence—on the teenager's shoulder along Market Street, for example, seemed, at the time, more truly an expression of the American capacity for rudeness; something worth deploring.

I will now admit the Japanese were prescient. Congestion aboard the 38 Geary turns the American toward Tokyo for civility. Headsets provide aural Nicorette for the duration; headsets provide alleviation from introspection or misanthropy. On the bus, the teenager and I sit so tightly packed our thighs touch. And yet we are transported as though separately, invisibly. I owe my solitude to Johannes Gutenberg (well, as does my seatmate; the Walkman is an extenuation of the book).

One does not relinquish one's identity for the duration of a ride on the 38, but one does allow one's purpose to slip its leash, to merge with the idea of civic order, which in this case is the idea of arriving safely at one's destination. Those who insist upon their identities, even on the 38 Geary, are cautiously regarded by other passengers as potentially dangerous.

But there are spires to observe and clouds, coats, briefcase interiors, flashes of privacy as potent as leitmotivs in an Edith Wharton story; eyes to avoid. There are conversations to overhear, newspapers, books to read:

> *Since I was not bewitched in adolescence*
> *And brought to love,*
> *I will attend to the trees and their gracious silence,*
> *To winds that move.*

Silencing Philip Larkin, a phone tweedles in someone's purse or pocket. And now it is Scandinavia's turn to chart a course for this crowded 38. Finland, a nation famous for sardines and suicide and short winter days, uses more cell phones, per capita, than any other country in the world. Everyone in the flaxen-haired capital of despair is on the phone, one hears.

And here, too, advertisements assure us of "connection," of never missing the call, of not wasting the moment, of being alive if only because the phone rings in the forest. To watch people on their phones in a crowd is to notice how disconnected they seem; how unprepared for solitude they seem. Neurosis, yes. Novelty is the American neurosis.

But to be forced to overhear the diary of a twit is still considered a foul. The other day in the elevator at the 450 Sutter Medical Building, a woman, oblivious of our overhearing, snarled to the mouthpiece of her cell phone that she was going to get an abortion and that was that.

Americans do not grant privacy to cell phone users. For one thing, the cell phoner insists on maintaining an "I" in situations where Americans have largely resigned themselves to taking their places in crowds and waiting to reemerge as singular.

I'm sure you have noticed joggers still do occupy private space in public America. Joggers can spit on the sidewalk, they run nearly nude, they pant, sweat, snort like dray horses. They are private, they are invisible. We understand they are *in ristauro* and in relation only to themselves, to their bodies, to "healthy activity." We do not stare.

The smoker invades our premises with every exhalation. There can be no privacy for him. We pass smokers on street corners and we ostentatiously wave our hands, clearing the landscape of pathology.

Many stores, restaurants, curiously, will blast music at us without permission and we make no objection, we do not wave our arms. Though I know a man from Berkeley who describes Dolby Sound as "intrusive," and regularly complains to theater managers about it.

We feel surrounded, that's the thing. Our borders do not hold. National borders do not hold. Ethnic borders. Religious borders. Aesthetic borders, certainly. Sexual borders. Allergenic borders. We live in the "Age of Diversity," in a city of diversity—I do, anyway—so we see what we do not necessarily choose to see: People listing according to internal weathers. We hear what we do not want to hear: Confessions we refuse to absolve.

Biology! That is what Franz Schurmann would call the bunch of us aboard the 38 Geary. I am on my way home from

lunch with Franz at our favorite dim sum restaurant, the aforementioned Mayflower—"no MSG." There we talked about our
usual subjects: Islam, China, the French Enlightenment. And
we talked about what Franz calls "biology."

In the Franz Schurmann lexicon (as, indeed, in his most recent book, *American Soul*), biology is a metaphor for life at
the bottom, or undifferentiated life: the crowd in the aisle, the
woman with her bag of tangerines, the girl with pure, I imagine
warm by this time, mountain water in a shipless plastic bottle
under her arm. All those school kids who won't slip off their
bulging backpacks and who stand in the aisles. The stew of humanity in Tokyo or Helsinki or aboard a San Francisco bus.
And, every once in a while, Americans are dragged to the bottom. The jury room. The army physical. The department of
motor vehicles. The emergency room. The United Airlines
ticket counter. The Last Judgment. Undifferentiated life is a
test of the American I, whereby each must figure out "the system" and seek her own advantage—must figure a way to get
the fuck out of here.

The "South" is another of Franz's metaphors—related to biology—in counterdistinction to the "North" (settled nations of
the Northern Hemisphere, the First World, where pale, rea-
sonable people speak quietly in large rooms about overpopulation). First Class. Business Class. The North is dependent
upon borders, restrictions, added tariffs, availability. The North
is also the State, all those who are on top—government plan-
ners, boards of directors, academicians, the politicians, managers, Founding Fathers, people with views, BMWs. Franz also
refers to the North as "physics."

The epic civilizations of Asia preoccupied Franz for most of his academic career—an august, a northerly career, it must be said—the vast movements of peoples preoccupied him; peasant revolutions, intricacies of aesthetic trod in the dust, the expendability of the single life, the disposition to eat anything that moves.

Now the famous sinologist, retired, spins the world over dim sum on a cold spring afternoon. Within his person Franz carries fifteen languages, tasselated literatures; memories of peasants, luminaries, terrains: The end of Ramadan and a mule ride through a mountain pass; volumes of yellow dust; a meal taken with dark, bearded men who squat to pluck gobbets of meat from a common platter while watchful women watch.

Franz's superiority over Francis Parkman is that Franz will attempt to answer any question put to him.

It is sometimes Franz's conceit that he is himself a peasant, of peasant mentality. "Where would the world be without peasants? Where would Chekhov be without peasants?" (. . . *The trees and their gracious silence.*)

Franz grew up in a working-class immigrant family in Hartford, Connecticut. As a boy he taped maps of the world to the walls of his bedroom to represent his heart's desire, which I take to be a desire for escape. The U.S. Army made Franz a translator, first-class, in Japan after the Second World War. The GI Bill sent him to Harvard.

Franz says he loved going to Harvard but he never really cared for academia; could not refrain from casting a peasant's eye upon the proceedings there; felt himself a sort of confidence man. Perhaps that is why, amid the steam and fishy roil of the Mayflower restaurant, Franz shares with me his intuition that the world is following his own inclination, or that his path partakes of a nose-diving zeitgeist: "The world is entering an era governed by biology, not the State." Borders are being trampled.

Before long, Franz has turned his regard from the round tables of Chinese families and from the waitress pushing her trolley of pork buns to consider the autocracy of his younger son, Peter, whose avocado must be pure. Enigmatic Peter lives harmlessly, delicately, behind a screen; is scrupulous; the seminarian son. In Peter's case, moral scruple has become dietary scruple. But what is it Peter will not swallow? Or what is the sacrament he seeks?

Peter yearns for cleansing. Where is the contaminant? Is it the great world Franz longed to join? In some sense Peter follows in his father's footsteps; sets off to see the world; displays a facility for languages. In some sense Peter considers himself to be a contaminant; seeks most the Zenish non-virtue of doing no harm. Though Franz can provide an approximate translation of Peter's behavior, its moment remains inexplicable to him. Despite Peter's care that his body not be defiled, his body is tattooed. Despite the impulse to live outside time, his mundane impulse to customize himself, to paint indelible bracelets on his arm, to embarrass some future version of himself with this illustration.

On the 38 Geary, a man sits picking his nose and rolls the gleaning between thumb and index finger into a pellet which he then examines. A young woman who sits opposite him stares with disbelief, involuntarily says out loud, "Eeeeeww." If she expects anyone to second her disgust, she is disappointed. The other passengers assume the man to be in his privacy or, at any rate, they maintain their own.

In the absence of morality agreed upon, in the absence of behavior agreed upon, we have streetlights, stop signs, crosswalks, courts of law, restraining orders. In the absence of streetlights, stop signs, courts of law, borders, morality agreed upon—all disregarded—Americans have decided we are surrounded, since we feel surrounded, by moral "space." Personal space. (The American version of an aura is not a superabundance of essence but is proscriptive, legal.) An inviolate space. A border. My space should not be violated by smoke or scent or chemical fume, by sound or sight or touch or sexual innuendo or prayer or immigrant. My space, moreover, should not be violated by authority—by parents, doctors, clergy, teachers.

A friend of mine, an English teacher at a local university, says he feels an obligation to point out to his students that the cigars in the canister on the mantelpiece in the Edith Wharton story are phallic symbols. But he is forbidden by his university to sit on the desk facing his students—a pose regarded by school governors as provocative. He could be charged with sexual harassment.

Against Christ's dictum that uncleanness does not come from without, but from within, there is this, from the program of a Shakespeare festival I attended last summer: *At the request of many audience members with environmental allergies, we ask you to be sparing in your use of scents.*

The local papers have run ads over the last few years for a housecleaning service that promises to rid one's home environment—draperies, furnace flues, carpets—of dust mites. The ads include a photograph of a microscopic dust mite, blown up to a proportion that puts one in mind of a balloon in the Macy's parade. The dust mite, an unfortunate airborne sprite, is crablike or toadlike; most resembles a smooth spread hand in a latex glove.

At the same time Americans have most come to mistrust, at least to joke about, spiritual guilt—to disregard the moral residue of behavior—we have come to internalize our mistrust of the environment in forms of paint chips, asbestos, food additives, sewage, corporate cynicism, arsenic, dust mites. The equanimity of environment to ourselves we call health. Our ability to match a nice day we call health, or to overmaster a gloomy day; our ability to handle our jobs and our chores and our money and our families we call health.

Ah, we are deeply impure! Because our environment is impure. Our religion concerns health more than morality—long life, and the dignity of the death we choose. But our bowels are impure. Our breasts. In the newspaper this morning, an op-ed: "Surely it is no coincidence that breast cancer rates have tripled since 1940. . . . We now know we can't trust anything the chemical companies tell us."

We are depressed. There is no "we" to that assertion, either. I am depressed. I feel impure. I feel that something is lost or wrong. Moreover, an ad on TV: "Get the buns you've always wanted!"

This would be laughable if there weren't, indeed, buns I've always wanted.

We perhaps no longer consider our bodies to be prisons of the spirit, temples, but microtechnology has displayed to us our bodies as ancient tablets or cave paintings—the genomes—hieroglyphics incised on the walls of cells, multicolored jump ropes, hangman's knots. Our irreducible element is not "I," as it turns out, but some ghostly "we," cumulative, remote—instructions that can be traced across the plains of Africa, all the way back to the finger of God.

Professor Faustus submits to a newsmaker interview on the "NewsHour"; assures us the Book of Life has been unlocked. But his smirk disquiets us.

As much as we are in thrall to health, we mistrust the clergy of that business. You know as well as I do that as soon as scientists can do something they will. They will clone. They will play knick-knack on your bones. We mistrust the liturgy of science: paper chasubles, disposable gloves, animal and human sacrifice, and all the pardons and plenary indulgences of HMOs. But even now, in the twenty-first century, scientists must eventually turn from the computer screen, from the Book of Life; must pull on latex gloves, must say "Let's just have a look." Science, even now, comes down to the digestive tract, to a finger inserted into your anus, to the triumph of biology, which is deeply humiliating to the American "I," and which is not, incidentally, sodomy, because there is no kindness to it, but only disgust.

This is the opposite of confession.

Christ, we notice, never said anything about a Book of Life. He did say the hairs on our heads were counted. He was easy enough in His skin to derive an illustration of morality from His familiarity with the human digestive tract.

▪ ▪ ▪

I noticed the woman withdraw from the reception line. She waited to be the last to approach me after a lecture I gave in a Congregational church in Pasadena. Her face, at one angle, described a Toltec carving. Then, a slight shift of her chin transported the eye to Kyoto. I had been speaking of brown— still, in truth, testing my own use of the term. The Japanese-Mexican woman had a brown story as well. She grew up feeling herself neither Japanese nor Mexican (because both), in a black neighborhood of Southern California.

But it was of her brother she needed to tell. Her brother went to jail because he was literally a misfit. Her brother felt himself culturally black, by which he meant in his gut, in his ear, in his soul, in his eye, in everything beyond and beneath his skin, but not in his skin. "The brothers," however, who were not his brothers, wanted nothing to do with him. Neither did the Asian gangs or the *norteños* who were preoccupied with fighting their own shadows. So he acted out, alone; tried to prove himself a reliable something by becoming an outlaw. In prison, the Mexican-Japanese brother became a reader, became a writer, entered the society of disembodied voices; sought, that way, to overmaster the competing claims of an impure ancestry by writing, at last, "I."

There is an aspect of symmetry we call loneliness. Two columns support an arch, creating emptiness. Leonardo's naked cartwheel of a man with hourly arms and legs and who describes an arc also describes loneliness. Wherever he puts his arms, they are empty. Do we derive our restlessness for symmetry from Nature—from outside ourselves—from geometry, from trees reflected in pools, or from our own bodies? There is a mystery of plurality about our bodies. The way we are constructed persuades us of duality, for we are halved, left, right.

We have two eyes, two ears, two nostrils. Nipples, arms, hands, legs, lungs, feet, testicles, ovaries. Parents. Where is the "I" in that? Language gives us the ability to address our selves. We have one brain (albeit when shelled as halved as walnut meats), mouth, throat, spinal cord, stomach, digestive tract, heart, navel, liver, sexual organ, anus. One memory. One stalk. It is the stalk that seems to yearn for complement. In E. M. Forster's novel *Maurice,* the hero has a dream: "Nothing happened. He scarcely saw a face, scarcely heard a voice say, 'that is your friend,' and then it was over, having filled him with beauty and taught him tenderness. . . ."

I meet teenagers—like the "Blaxican" in Riverside or the "Baptist Buddhist" in Atlanta—I meet them everywhere, at every gathering I attend, people who tell me they grew up alone. Because they didn't belong. Because they belong to too many. (The way we are constructed constructs introspection since we feel ourselves plural. Mirrors will cut us in two.) An African-American woman I met at a wedding told me that when she was a girl in Texas her best friend demanded of her, who was that white woman I saw you walking with? The white woman was her grandmother.

Then there is the forthright humor of my correspondent, the aforementioned Jewish-Muslim in San Jose, who by way of summation deadpans: "Most people I meet think I must be a frugal terrorist." My correspondent indirectly refers to the American Joke Book, which has a category devoted to miscegenation, to "crossing," as in: What do you get when you cross a Jew with a gay?

(A musical.) I understand. I sympathize, though I tend to withhold my brownest commiseration so as not to give offense.

A high school student, precocious, the most winning combination of Huck and Kerouac, visited me the other day for an interview. (I am his senior essay.) The kid was unshy and unsophisticated both. Unblinking. Seventeen and he had hitched solo across the continent. He said it was cool with him that I was gay but he wanted to know how I measured the influence of homosexuality . . . *on your writing, since you never say.*

(I remember my father regularly remarking—I hadn't realized I was listening—how in Mexico a person is guilty until proven innocent; whereas in the United States, the opposite faith prevails. I've never met a more law-abiding man than my father so I don't know why this legal inversion interested him so much. To this day, I believe both, more or less, because one is more than one. One embodies contradiction through time. And though the man may turn against an earlier number—the old man, for example, regretting an adolescent kiss or a rock thrown or a blue tattoo—that regret is also a kind of reconciliation because it is an acknowledgment of linkage. What makes me brown is that I live with both Napoleonic and Anglo-Saxon notions of guilt and innocence, not my skin. I do not reconcile.)

It's true, I never say. I replied to the young man's request for candor cryptically. Walt Whitman, I said. Whitman's advantage was that—prohibited from admitting the specific—he learned to speak of the many. Or. In order to disguise his love of the singular Other, he had to compose an anthem to an entire nation. Of every hue and caste am I, he sang, while the heterosexual nation tore itself asunder as blue or gray.

The young man said something wonderful in response. He said his father worked for a corporation that had transported his family from one identical suburb to another across America, north to south, to Marietta, Georgia: "When our family lived in Georgia, whenever I'd see a black man and a white man walking down the street together, I'd always assume they were gay."

■ ■ ■

We sometimes confuse ourselves with outcome and call history "destiny." If a man dies on the gallows, we may cross ourselves and say to ourselves he was born to die. So are we all.

If a man dies unhappily, we are likely to say he had an unhappy life. That is not necessarily so.

Or, we may say of someone, she made her bed, now she must lie in it, which is not necessarily true. She did not, perhaps, choose the life she lies in. Perhaps she chose a smile.

Perhaps the American "I" is not truly individualistic, as Paolo noticed. But the American "I" is predicated upon the astonishing "pursuit of happiness," truly an American invention. But what if one "I" is Roman Catholic and one "I" is gay? Down which path is happiness pursued?

I never say. I am often enough asked how it is I call myself a gay Catholic. A paradox? Does the question betray a misunderstanding of both states? No, not really. What you are asking is how can I be an upstanding one and the other. When you slice an avocado, the pit has to go with one side or the other, doesn't it? Weighting one side or the other. A question about the authenticity of the soul, I suppose. Or the wishbone—some little tug-of-war; some tension.

The tension I have come to depend upon. That is what I mean by brown. The answer is that I cannot reconcile. I was born a Catholic. Is homosexuality, then, a conversion experience? No. I was born gay. Is Catholicism ever a choice? Yes.

No. Not at first. I embraced Catholicism without question. It was the air, it was the light. Years later, I came to Catholicism in deliberation, defeat—satirically, perhaps—nevertheless on my knees. How else to approach a church established for losers, for a kingdom not of this world, a kingdom of fools? Whatever faith I confess is based upon my certainty that I can do nothing. I can save no one. I do not wish to live beyond a crucifix. The crucifix does not represent guilt to me, but love.

I well understand the wish to be quit of the church. Those old men sitting in a row through centuries—back, back, to a roomful of frightened men, of purposes varied and apprehensions varied. Their paper hats. Do they wish me harm? Some do. Some rescue. I kiss their hands for they do not relinquish what they hold, what they pass forward. That which is homosexual in me most trusts the durability of this non-blood lineage. *Trees and their gracious silence.* Though I scorn them sometimes too and I ask forgiveness for my scorn. For none of us has made flesh.

■ ■ ■

By brown I mean love.

The brownest rendition of love I can summon is the Sermon on the Mount, that plein-air toss of ambiguous bread. All paradox is brown and divine paradox is browner than which no browner can be conceived.

The brownest secular essay I know is the one called *La Raza Cósmica* by José Vasconcelos, a Mexican who wrote in 1925:

> The days of pure whites, the victors of today, are as numbered as the days of their predecessors. Having fulfilled their destiny of mechanizing the world, they themselves have set, without knowing it, the basis for the new period: The period of the fusion and mixing of all peoples.

This is not the same as saying "the poor shall inherit the earth" but is possibly related. The poor shall overrun the earth. Or the brown shall.

Many Americans opt for a centrifugal view of the future, a black-and-white version—I don't mean skin but cultural intransigence—deduced from history as hatred. A future of real armies ranged on opposing sides of a cultural divide—Muslims and Hindus, say. But in our postmodern, post-everything world, the competing armies—theologies, tribes—I think might as likely assemble within a single breast. The result of love. Can what love has bound together as flesh be reconciled? The traditional task of marriage is to make flesh. The Indian, the ash blond, stir, make flesh.

Perhaps my parents became one by creating my flesh, but I may have a problem with it: It was the grandson of an observant Jew, a young man who feared he was irrelevant to history; who, on the anniversary of Hitler's birthday, pulled on a long dark raincoat, in the style of a comic-book avenger, secreted several rifles beneath his long coat, burst into his high school cafeteria; opened fire. He is dead now. His life is over.

We of the twenty-first century may be headed for a desire for cleansing, of choosing, of being one thing or another. The brown child may grow up to war against himself. To attempt to be singular rather than several. May seek to obliterate a part of himself. May seek to obliterate others.

(I reopen this book in the terrible dusk of September 11, 2001. On that day, several medieval men in the guise of multicultural America and in the manner of American pop culture, rode dreadnoughts through the sky. These were men from a world of certainty, some hours distant—a world where men presume to divine, to enforce, to protectively wear the will of God; a world where men wage incessant war against the impurity that lies without [puritans!] and so they mistrust, they wither whatever they touch; they have withered the flower within the carpet they have walked upon. These several in-authentic men, of fake I.D., of brutish sentimentality, went missing from U.S. immigration rolls, were presumed lost and assimilated into brown America, these men of certainty re-fused to be seduced by modernity, postmodernity; by what I have been at pains to describe as brown, as making.)

The headmaster walking me down a long corridor on that day I spoke at a high school in Los Angeles, admitted, as we drew near the assembly room, that most of his students are bored by talk of "diversity"; are impious toward that word. "It's the parents who are eager for their kids to learn about multi-culturalism."

The parent's complaint: The working-class father purchased his daughter a computer, because (he told me) he wanted to give his daughter the world. (He believed the television commercial.) Whereupon the daughter logged into chatrooms crowded with people only exactly like herself.

Teachers tell me their students are "beyond race, don't think about it the way we do." Other teachers tell me cafeteria tables sort as reliably as ever and according to every conceivable bor-der: color, jock, slut, nerd, born-again, heavy metal, rap. Both descriptions must be true.

Remember where you came from. Such is not our way. Who can say that anymore in America? As lives meet, chafe, there will be a tendency to retreat. When the line between us is unenforced or seems to disappear, someone will surely be troubled and nostalgic for straight lines and will demand that the future give him the fundamental assurance of a border.

A thought that haunts many African Americans I know is that they are the same distance from the slave owner as from the slave. Both strains have contributed to their bodies, to their waking spirits. I am the same distance from the conquistador as from the Indian. Righteousness should not come easily to any of us.

Perhaps she chose a smile.

Perhaps she kept the appointment for an eye examination. Perhaps the examining technician reached to adjust the overhead lamp. He did this in some way so as to suggest the competence of an athlete or the thinness of a matador's waist—he somehow surpassed himself in the gesture—a gesture so thorough that she could seem to inhabit it for the eternity of one moment, rather like the Virgin in the painting of the Annunciation; the overwhelming competence of the angel. It was only one of thousands of involuntary responses to any given moment. Except at that moment he smiled.

She turns from the painting of the Annunciation in tears. Her sinuses have dilated, spoiling the taste of the gum. She locates the rest room. She pauses at the case full of swords. She recoils from her imagination of their sharpness. She looks at her watch. She exits the museum. She needs an abortion. The angel was married.

▪   ▪   ▪

It remains for me to tell you the outcome of Franz's deliberation. He purchased the organic avocado. Of course he did. Finally, it made no difference to him one way or the other.

Something that passes into the sewer. It was getting late, getting dark.

So Peter remains undefiled at his father's hands. From India, Peter e-mailed his father an account of a recurring dream, a dream of returning to a Tibetan village where he spent a part of last year. A dream of walking up into the mountain—above the tree line—where footprints disappear, where the wind dies, where his dreaming self or spirit seems not to be separate from the white air, the white air not separate from the snow he walks upon. A dream of purification? Franz took it as such. A dream of reconciling.

They say, people who have had near-death experiences say, who have floated above their bodies prone on gurneys in operating rooms or at the sites of accidents, that reentering their bodies—a drumroll; the steep dive once more into their meat—was painful and repellent to them, to their disembodied selves.

Thud. My eyes are open. It is four-thirty in the morning, one morning, and my dry eyes click in their sockets, awake before the birds. There is no light. The eye strains for logic, some play of form. I have been dreaming of wind. The tree outside my window stands silent. I listen to the breathing of the man lying beside me. I know where I am. I am awake. I am alive. Am I tethered to earth only by this fragile breath? A strawful of breath at best. Yet this is the breath that patients beg, their hands gripping the edges of mattresses; this is the breath that wrestles trees, that brings down all the leaves in the Third Act. We know where the car is parked. We know, word-for-word, the texts of plays.

We have spoken, in proximity to one another, over years, sentences, hundreds of thousands of sentences—bright, grave, fallible, comic, perishable—perhaps eternal? I don't know. Where does the wind go? When will the light come?

We will have hotcakes for breakfast.

How can I protect this . . . ?

My church teaches me I cannot. And I believe it. I turn the pillow to its cool side. Then rage fills me, against the cubist necessity of having to arrange myself comically against orthodoxy, against having to wonder if I will offend, against theology that devises that my feeling for him, more than for myself, is a vanity. My brown paradox: The church that taught me to understand love, the church that taught me well to believe love breathes—also tells me it is not love I feel, at four in the morning, in the dark, even before the birds cry.

Of every hue and caste am I.

Acknowledgments

THE IDEA FOR A BOOK ABOUT HISPANICS IN AMERICA WAS proposed to me by my literary agent and friend, Georges Borchardt. It was he and Lourdes Lopez at the Borchardt Agency who were the first readers of this book which ventures afield.

During the years I spent thinking about the color brown, conversations with artists and poets and sociologists and friends helped direct my writing. I remain indebted to more persons than I can remember here, but to these certainly: Nell Altizer, Will Homisak, Joe Loya, Dominic Martello, Mark Scott, David Reid, Michael Goldberg, Charles Eissfeldt, Paul Holdengraber, Franz Schurmann, Paolo Polledri, Seymour Martin Lipset, David Ligare, and Michael Lawson. I owe special gratitude to Sandy Close, the executive editor of the Pacific News Service and my co-conspirator of many years. And I remain indebted to Kathryn Court, my editor at Viking Penguin. Finally, I acknowledge the assistance of the Archive of the Metropolitan Opera and the Public Relations Office of the Stanford University Athletic Department.

I am also indebted to a book browning on my shelf. I could not have written this book without the precedent of William

Gass's *On Being Blue: A Philosophical Inquiry.* His blue put me in mind of brown, of isolating brown. Truly, one way to appreciate the beauty of the world is to choose one color and to notice its recurrence in rooms, within landscapes. And upon bookshelves.